CAN WE HAVE THE
CONVERSATION?

A Spiritual Multicultural Approach to Racial Reconciliation

BRENDA DARBY, MA

ISBN:

Cover Design by Justin Trammell

Dedication

This book is dedicated to my loving husband, Fred, who
taught me a love for the Word of God; to my loving
parents, Warner and Laura Humble, who are deceased;
to my brother, Kevin; to my grandparents, Joseph and
Maggie Ford; and to my great-grandmother, Mary
Thurston, who could not read or write but taught me to
sing the songs about our God and the songs of freedom
while she was alive. We sang them together.

This book is also dedicated to my friend
Sharon Randles, wife of Lyle Randles.
Lyle and I were having the conversation before he died.

"TELL ME HOW MUCH YOU KNOW

OF THE SUFFERINGS OF

YOUR FELLOW HUMANS,

AND I WILL TELL YOU

HOW MUCH

YOU HAVE LOVED THEM."

—Helmut Thielicke

CONTENTS

FOREWORD

By Lyle Randles

There are, regrettably, quite a few unfortunate stains recorded in the chronicles of American history that bring disgrace
upon our nation. For example, our interaction with the Native
American was (and in some cases, remains) a most unpleasant
affair. One might also point to our mistreatment of Asians,
originally imported in an effort to circumvent labor shortages,
but then placed underfoot and marginalized for generations.
And of course, our greatest (and longest-lasting) blemish pertains to that of the American Negro.

As Brenda observes, any review of the American Negro's
plight must begin in Africa herself, for it is in our observation
of the entire experience that we might best begin to understand
the depth of the wounds suffered as well as the degree of diffi-
culty we face when attempting to reconcile White and Black.

Writing as I am from a Christian perspective, I am both
intrigued and touched by Brenda's thoughts concerning the
obvious need for reconciliation. But it is when I look at the
issue over such a great breadth of history that I ask, "Where has
the church been throughout this period of struggle and strife?"

History teaches us that White America struggled severely
over the issue of slavery. But unfortunately, we also prospered
from the arrangement. Slavery became the financial engine that
helped this country reach its manifest destiny, and in the final
analysis, it was our pocketbooks that ended up ruling any sense
of moral outrage that may have come forth from the church.

I find it incredibly interesting that as the struggle rose to a peak, virtually every Christian denomination split over the issue of slavery. In a country that was already multi-denominational, we witnessed a doubling in those same denominations within a very short period of time. Clearly, the forces driving slavery itself had an enormous influence on our brothers and sisters of the past.

Yet, as White America struggled, God was at work among the slaves. The Gospel of our Lord was not only being proclaimed to the American Negro, but great numbers of slaves were declaring their loyalty and devotion to Jesus. I believe it impossible to ascertain the percentage of slaves that ultimately proclaimed their faith in Christ, but they eventually became the most highly Christianized segment of our society.

By the end of the Civil War, Americans (both Black and White) were exhausted. For reasons that continue to be debated even today, our society tore and gouged at itself until our nation was almost torn in two. The conflict produced well over 600,000 casualties (3 percent of our total population), and upon cessation of hostilities, almost 4 million slaves were displaced. Those that did not become sharecroppers upon land carved out of former plantations were dispersed either north or west.

It must be kept in mind at this point in the narrative that these ex-slaves were, for the greatest part, an illiterate and agrarian people who had little or no education. Moreover, they were released into a society that made it abundantly clear that they were not welcome. As with almost every other people group that had immigrated to our country, the American Negro immediately took up their position on the bottom rung of America's economic ladder, taking almost any means of support they could find. However, unlike almost every other people group that had immigrated to our country, the American Negro was, for the most part, kept near the bottom of that ladder, and there the descendants of those former slaves struggle to find economic equality even to this day.

After countless decades of suffering as slaves, the American Negro entered the post–Civil War era as a free but rejected citizen. Any sense of celebration at the conclusion of the conflict was probably short lived, for it did not take long for the largely White population to communicate their unwillingness to treat Black Americans as equals.

From my perspective, this failure on the part of a largely Christian nation represents a low watermark in American history. There were no social service agencies within the U.S. government in the mid-nineteenth century. Nor were state governments equipped to aid Black Americans. Within the context of that era, the church served as the social safety net within our society. But where was the church?

Though freed by a presidential proclamation with liberties and rights extended through constitutional amendments, the American Negro felt, for the most part, abandoned and rejected by a country they now called home. As a result, Blacks developed what Brenda refers to as an attitude of resistance and suspicion. Coupled with a healthy dose of cultural paranoia, the American Negro retreated into his own culture—a culture within a culture, if you will. Refusing to identify with the majority culture, Blacks began to develop an alternate set of values.

Though Civil Rights legislation of the 1960s went a long way toward normalizing the American Negro in the eyes of the law, nothing of substance has been able to dismantle the barriers of rejection and distrust that seem to permeate African-American communities all around our country today.

But the solution is not so easily found. It is not a matter for politicians to address. This is not a situation that can be legislated away. Nor can we break down barriers through speeches or large-scale attempts to seek one another's forgiveness. From a purely biblical perspective, we must begin the arduous journey to recovery by simply loving one another.

Let us not forget Jesus's parable concerning the Good Samaritan. The rift between Jew and Samaritan was significant. Jews looked down on Samaritans as being unworthy half-breeds. Yet it was a Samaritan who stopped to help the wounded man, not the priest or the Levite.

Though churchgoing Christians have undoubtedly heard numerous references to this parable over the course of their lives, we have somehow been unable to discern how the parable applies to us. The American Negro was that wounded man on the side of the road. But both Southerner and Northerner passed him by.

When are we, the church of Jesus Christ, going to stop and kneel beside our wounded brother? After all, he never asked to come to this country, and he certainly didn't ask to suffer through the injustices of slavery.

And doesn't this question become all the more weighty when we consider that the man at the side of the road is more likely than not our brother in Christ?

So where do we begin?

4

ACKNOWLEDGMENTS

First of all, I give thanks to my Lord and Savior, Jesus Christ, for allowing me to bring this project to completion. This is a thank-you to those who gave me the impetus to write the book. After the loss of my husband, Fred, I don't know how long it would have taken me to pick up my master's thesis and begin again. A hearty thank-you goes to Lyle Randles, who worked with me chapter by chapter until his death. Lyle and I were having the conversation together. Words of appreciation and gratitude are extended to those who see me as a gift to the Body of Christ and strive to see me live to my potential and join me on the journey: I say Thank You. In my heart, I am grateful for the precious memories and discussions as we sorted out our past and addressed reconciliation, the church, and the race issue. I give thanks to those who pray for me, those who have supported and encouraged me, those who have shared with me and cried with me. Thanks to those who have laughed with me and at me. I give thanks to the Lord for Precious, the little girl inside of me, who continues to raise her head and be known.

Lord, may the words of this book be acceptable unto you. Oh Lord! My Savior and Redeemer.

PREFACE

Sophie's Story

There is an old story about a little girl whose mother had died. The little girl's name was Sophie. After her mother's funeral services, Sophie remained behind at the cemetery, wondering how her mother would ever find her way home. The funeral assistant smiled and gave Sophie some popcorn kernels, telling her to periodically drop a kernel of popcorn on the ground as she made her way back home, and that in so doing, she would create a trail of kernels that her mother could easily follow.

Though, in reality, Sophie's mother would no longer be with her, a closer look with our spiritual imagination shows us that these popcorn kernels were a strong reminder of the connection between Sophie and her mother. This connection would not be broken by any tragedy—not even by death. They also represent a journey of hope for those searching for a place of acceptance and affirmation. For us in the believing community, it is a journey of intimacy and reconciliation with our God.

This anecdotal story captures the emotion of the real-life faith journey of African-American Christians in the United States. Torn from family and country, forsaken in a strange land, African-Americans have been on a long journey "home," searching for reunification in some way with all that was lost. In much the same way that Sophie dropped popcorn kernels in the hope of reuniting with her mother, we African-Americans have been clinging to the "Seeds of Hope" that God has been dropping into our hearts as we search to somehow regain what was stolen from us. We seek to find acceptance within new surroundings—seeds of hope that, unlike Sophie's kernels, will lead us home.

Though this pilgrimage is far from over, we can look back and see a long trail of kernels that bear witness to the faithfulness of God and to the resilience of African-Americans over the centuries. Yet, even within this resilience, life taunts us inwardly by wounds of peril, loss, and suffering we experience in the various spheres[1] of our society. These wounds have hindered the healing process of the average African-American in so many ways, leaving much of this population disconnected and isolated from mainstream America.

This book is about that painful journey—but it is also about those "Seeds of Hope." It is about how we might go about healing the spiritual damage that *racism* and the history of slavery have caused us. Here we define racism as "a learned belief in racial superiority, which includes the belief that race determines intellectual, cultural, and moral capacities. The practice of racism includes both racial prejudice and discrimination against others based on their race and ethnicity."[2] Further, this book is about the misinformation or misunderstanding of many Americans, not just African-Americans, about the biblical concept of "Life in the Spirit."[3] As we move forward, we will look at the biblical concept of Spiritual Formation—how it connects to the experience of African-Americans, and to the experience of African-American Christians in particular, as they interact with the dominant culture. One of the goals of the Spiritual Formation movement, and the goal promoted most often in our modern culture, is to provide healing for *individual and group* transformation. Yet, when we study African-American history, we awaken to the fact that what we really need is transformation of our *whole community and nation*. Racism has left scars both internal and external—scars on the individual, scars on the family, scars on the culture, scars on society, and scars on the church as a whole.

All need healing.

—Brenda Darby

INTRODUCTION

Recorded in the Hall of Records of Louisa County, Virginia, is the purchase of several men and women of the Thurston Plantation. This is the origin of my family, and the beginning of my story. Like so many others, my family's emancipation from slavery occurred through the Thirteenth Amendment. Then, their arduous task of scratching out a life began.

I attended church throughout my childhood, but did not come to real faith until much later in life. Like many African-American young people, I was just looking for a place to fit in, where I would be accepted and affirmed.

As I grew and entered the workforce, I continued to see my brothers and sisters in the workforce mistreated, overlooked, and isolated in both the governmental and private sectors. I attended in-house seminars and workshops and partook in sensitivity sessions. Yet I continued to hurt, for myself and for my race. I believe my passion for the younger generation was the impetus for my joining the YWCA Big Sister program. I wanted to help young African-Americans learn the "system," have a place to vent their woes, and avoid labels, such as "Uncle Tom," in the process. All of this was "outside" of Christ and Christ's church. It would be years before I would knowingly have an encounter with God.

I had friends who worked hard in the faith and for their local churches. I would even attend their church events, and travel with them. Still I had no concern for my soul. Eventually, a series of hard experiences and losses humbled me, and the light of Christ burst in upon my heart.

I will revisit the subject of my own journey again in the afterword ("Soulful Reflections"), where I hope to provide the reader with a snapshot of how the love of God now compels me to serve Him, even as the Spirit continues to peel away the outer layers of this crusty old artichoke of a saint.

I mention my personal journey here because it is worth remembering that everyone has a story of redemption. Everyone is on a journey.

For many African-American Christians, the journey to heal the interior wounds of racism and oppression is also a journey to find our identity. Understanding our history is foundational to understanding ourselves. Because we are part of the body of believers, this journey must involve our brothers and sisters of other races—we do not journey alone. In order for the interior and personal wounds to heal, the exterior and communal wounds need healing as well.

If we are to love like Jesus, it will require the whole Body of Christ to gather to "have the conversation." This is necessary if healing is to take place. There is just that much at stake for our nation and the world. Here Sophie drops a kernel of popcorn. We all have to study our history, and together we have to have the conversation. The past needs scrutiny and understanding; together we can redeem the time.

Just as the Lord spoke to Jeremiah, so too His words resonate with us today:

> For thus says the LORD:…I visit you, and I will fulfill to you my promise and bring you back to this place. For surely I know the plans I have for you, says the LORD, plans for your welfare and not for harm, to give you a future with hope. Then when you call upon me and come and pray to me, I will hear you. When you search for me, you will find me; if you seek me with all your heart.
>
> —JEREMIAH 29:10-13, NRSV

It is my prayer that you will discover a divine trail of popcorn kernels, just like Sophie and me, leading you home—a place where love prevails. Though the story you tell and the path you walk are undoubtedly different from mine, I suspect that you will discover a path littered with spiritual kernels. My prayer is that this book can be yet one more of those kernels that serves to secure you in the everlasting arms of our Savior. Reflective questions have been included at the end of each chapter to stir your consciousness and your heart. I wonder what thoughts and memories you will sift through.

ONE

History to Learn, Questions to Answer

So if anyone is in Christ, there is a new creation: everything old has passed away; see, everything has become new! All this is from God, who reconciled us to himself through Christ, and has given us the ministry of reconciliation; that is, in Christ God was reconciling the world to himself, not counting their trespasses against them, and entrusting the message of reconciliation to us. So we are ambassadors for Christ, since God is making his appeal through us; we entreat you on behalf of Christ, be reconciled to God.

—2 CORINTHIANS 5:17-20, NRSV

IN THIS BOOK, I am trying to explore, from a cultural and historical point of view, the spiritual factors that have shaped the psyche and attitude of African-Americans. These factors have played a major role in Spiritual Formation, yet for many of us, the negative aspects of our internal realities remain unaddressed and continue to be a nemesis to our spiritual growth and maturity. Looking at the issue from a formational perspective will allow us to identify several factors that plague our culture overall. Then we can see how government, society, and the church have had an impact on our lifestyles.

Let us start here. This book is intended to be more than just an historical account—it is intended to be a balanced global view of the African-American journey that addresses the cultural uniqueness of the African-American's diaspora. When I began the research for this book, I was disappointed at the amount of material that was at my disposal. It seemed that African-American scholars were not writing for the academic institutions in this area. The good news is that the momentum is shifting and a movement exists to gather all contemplative people of color together and to begin to chronicle our journey from a spiritual perspective. This movement is brewing all across the nation, and it is providing us the chance for a new and improved approach toward spiritual transformation that is informative, that heals, and that reconciles—both now and for future generations.

A lack of resources showed me there was a need for this book—a book that I hope will begin to change lives for the better. In the midst of my search for knowledge, I realized that God had given me a passion to learn and a desire for authenticity. I sensed the Lord leading me to start my search in Africa. So, I eagerly accepted this mission! I embarked on a study of African religions and traditions during pre-slavery times. Understanding these African traditions was crucial to drawing an accurate picture of the African-American historical and social context. An audited class on African Theology reinforced my approach and caused me to narrow the focus of this manuscript. Through this writing, I bore witness, in a more intimate way, to the richness of the African tribal system of community. The historical traditions that have flourished over the centuries were deeply rooted within the souls of the African people and of their American descendants. As I researched, I marveled at the ability of enslaved Africans, forced against their will into a new land, to nurture and care for one another in spite of the oppression and racism they encountered and endured. Even revisiting the slave narratives was difficult, but in between the stories and the songs, I saw God at work in their experiences, and they did too.

God's grace covered my laborious, self-assigned course of reading. Through the pain and suffering of my ancestors, I saw hope, driven by the will to live and strive. Yes, I shed tears during my research—tears that said, "Thank you for staying alive," to the early slaves who believed we could be free. There were tears that bore witness to missed opportunity, isolation, and abandonment. There were tears as I remembered repeating those same lifestyle experiences. Then, there were tears of joy that surfaced as I witnessed my ancestors' accomplishments in this nation—the amazing victories they were able to achieve in the midst of all the challenges. I can hear them singing the gospel song, "We Shall Overcome."

Will you join me on this multifaceted landscape of a journey of transformation? I want to share the history I have learned and the tools I have gathered. I want this book to become a resource in the hands of the church—a resource that helps to transform all the people of God everywhere.

God is unchangingly good, and God always has been with us, even in the days of our painful past.

THE AFRICAN-AMERICAN STORY

My story is just one of countless stories from within the African-American community. To understand fully the saga of my people and their trials while pursuing freedom and racial equality, we cannot begin our journey by merely looking at a single life, or even the lives of an entire generation. This book will outline major highlights from the history of the African-American experience. Our journey must begin on the shores of West Africa with thousands upon thousands of Africans sold into slavery. In light of the affliction, we can see kernels of divine intervention that began to loosen the yokes of bondage for individuals and families.

We will explore African spirituality and delve briefly into the rich culture, traditions, and belief systems of its people during the late 1700s. It is through this cultural lens that we will begin to understand better the development of African-American worldviews.

The journey will continue through the Civil War, the era of Reconstruction, World Wars I and II, the economic collapse of the nation during the Depression, the fight for civil rights, and all the way up to our current-day crises.

RECLAIMING OUR TRADITIONS

The journey of African-Americans is replete with tales of economic deprivation, social institutionalization, and overt racism. Yet African-Americans learned to survive due in part to a heritage grounded in community and nurturing relationships. Within the African traditions is a sense of strong community connectedness, i.e., soul care. This part of our heritage we must reclaim.

THE FOUR WOUNDS

One thing that I saw in my research was the clear effects of four cultural conditioning factors[4] on African-American life. For this treatise the terms "cultural conditioning factors" and "wounds" are used interchangeably. They are:

1. Identity
2. Sacred Secrets
3. Powerlessness/Rage
4. Mistrust[5]

Once we identify the four wounds, the remedies for our conditioning become clear:

- We must reconcile ourselves to God through the Word of God and the spiritual disciplines of Spiritual Formation to regain our footing.

- We must reconcile ourselves to our history by reclaiming our cultural traditions (especially those of community and song).

After these, we can show neighbor-love to each other and begin to reconcile ourselves to one another by beginning to "have the conversation."

One of the most important books I discovered in my quest was *Beyond the Suffering*, by Dr. Robert W. Kelleman and Karole A. Edwards, which chronicles the facets of spiritual direction, soul care during slavery, and the importance of rehearsing our rich heritage within families and to others. I sought to capitalize on this writing and expound upon the conditioning factors mentioned above that stem from that experience and which, in reality, are still a part of the African-American psyche today. My investigative reading became grounds for healing from the psychological effects of slavery that I still wrestled with myself. I have seen a few things. My sensitivity to the remarks and gestures of others was heightened. Subtle nuances revealed my cultural traps and exposed my own personal rage and racial tendencies. These reminders drove me to prayer.

As I will discuss in later chapters of this book, I discovered through my research that the African-Americans feelings of resistance, suspicion, and lack of trust have historical justification. There are legitimate reasons why we have felt the need to make and maintain a separate culture within a culture, and those reasons have much to do with the wrong done to us.

CONNECTIONS WITH OTHER CULTURAL JOURNEYS

This book is not only an overview of the African-American journey, but also an opportunity to observe the multidimensional spirituality of mankind and the effects of the Fall as evidenced through the building of this country via the engine of slavery. Even a cursory review of American history will serve to underscore the depths of human depravity (whether people acted consciously or unconsciously) and will underscore the truth that without a connection to God, the populace is ill prepared to address the inner scars of self or of a fallen society. Yet, there lies within all human consciousness the quest for "coherence and purpose to life and one's identity."[6] Still, there is more. Let us not forget the need for love, acceptance, and affirmation that lies at the core of all humankind. Irrespective of one's ethnicity or cultural background, we all seem to seek fulfillment from something outside of ourselves. At times it seems that humankind (indeed, all of creation) has been subjected to futility, yet within each human heart lies a hope that all will be set free from the corruption of this world into some unknown yet glorious state of freedom…when all will live as God first intended.

> For I consider that the sufferings of this present time are not worthy to be compared with the glory that is to be revealed to us. For the anxious longing of the creation waits eagerly for the revealing of the sons of God. For the creation was subjected to futility, not willingly, but because of Him who subjected it, in hope that the creation itself also will be set free from its slavery to corruption into the freedom of the glory of the children of God.
>
> —ROMANS 8:18-21, NASB

Within every people group, there exist biases toward people of other races, ethnicities, and religions. The journey of African-Americans can be viewed as unique when compared to other cultures in America. This book does not take the view that racial bias, in the end, produces a culture of African-Americans as victims. This is not the end of our story. Quite the contrary: one of the chief aims of this book is to help African-Americans view themselves as victorious.

Many other ethnic groups have suffered oppression and prejudice as they have attempted to assimilate into American culture. This has had generational implications and haunted the very fiber of the culture at large. Therefore, we cannot conclude that African-Americans are the sole party injured by the majority culture. Many people and people groups suffer wrongs and exposure to biases and racial indignities that have shaped their lives. They have endured similar struggles while trying to establish a foothold in American society. It is my intention to expose the victimization and persecution that reaches not only from African to American culture but also from other cultures to American culture. We are not alone.

It is also important to note that this discourse does not focus on faultfinding. In essence, I want to present a global perspective of a nation developing in the midst of turmoil and to show how that course of development had an impact on generation upon generation of African-Americans. I will not be addressing the relationship between African-Americans and other subcultures. I will focus on the impact of the dominant White culture upon African-Americans and how the relationship between the two serves to shape both the culture and the spirituality of Black Americans.

SPIRITUAL FORMATION

Written to and for African-Americans, as well as the believing community, this discourse intends to expose the scars left by wounds that have gone untreated for generations. As part of a prescription to treat those wounds, we will explore the principles of Spiritual Formation. By definition, Spiritual Formation is a "means of grace through which God conforms us to the image of Christ for the sake of others."[7] It is in this relationship where Jesus tends to the longings of our hearts, hears our cries, and accompanies us through the journey of life. He plants His seeds of hope, while reshaping the clutter in our minds and transforming our hearts. This is true intimacy. My own personal experiences during my studies at Biola University proved to be an opportunity for renewed awareness that led to transformation. I began to understand how the biblical ideologies of Spiritual Formation search the deep issues of the heart and lead to inner healing. These biblical principles so move me that I want to share these spiritual disciplines with others.

Today we might view this kind of intimacy as "soul care." David Benner describes caring for souls as "support and restoration of the well-being of persons in their depth and totality, with particular concern for their inner life."[8] Benner further describes this concept of care as "actions that are designed to support the well-being of something or someone…and cure [that] which refers to actions that are designed to restore well-being that has been lost."[9]

As in the case of Sophie, one could not cure her hurt, but one could certainly care for her soul.

HAVING THE CONVERSATION

My goal is to bring light to truths that heal and liberate the soul. In doing so, I hope to highlight the historical, cultural, and psychological affects that shape the psyche of African-American communities. The key aspects of these cultural conditioning factors are vital to any discussion that will lead to reconciliation. I can only hope that the result of my effort will give rise to countless conversations between peoples of different colors, cultures, and ethnicities. History chronicles man's inhumanity to man. Lest we forget, there is the mistreatment of the American Indian in the early stages of this country's expansion. With World War II came the Holocaust, the genocide of over 8 million European Jews during the reign of Adolf Hitler. While Hitler was wreaking havoc in Europe, in 1942, the Japanese forces bombed Pearl Harbor. The fear of espionage sparked President Franklin D. Roosevelt to sign Executive Order 9066, which authorized the detention of over 100,000 Japanese American citizens and Japanese residents into internment camps. Lastly, let us not forget the hate crimes against Muslims after 9/11. There is much work to be done.

It is important to note that all of these avenues of healing are essential. First, learning and discussing our history brings us to the table, thus creating the impetus for having the conversation as we together share our stories. Second, the formational aspect of the spiritual practices helps us to find God in our story. It is here where the Word of God is preeminent and can usher us into deeper truths. It is also here that the church plays a major role in the transformation process by discipling the Body of Christ and preparing the ground so that change can take place—if, indeed, it ever is going to begin. Nevertheless, despite our willingness or unwillingness to come to the table, the church was and is, and always will be, the necessary context for spiritual healing. For with God, all things are possible.

As Paul says in the New Testament verses from 2 Corinthians that open this chapter, we are ambassadors (whether we like it or not) and ours is the ministry of reconciliation. This is the work of the Holy Spirit. I did not want a book just to reflect Black/White issues, but also to reflect the varied belief systems at work in the hearts of humankind and the need to come together. Theologically and spiritually separated is the Body of Christ. How do we bring about reconciliation under these circumstances? What can bring unification to the Body of Christ in these socially inclusive times? Should we not be like the tribe of "Issachar, men who understood the times" (1 Chronicles 12:32a, NIV)?

Maybe if we were more inclusive and talked about such matters more openly, both individuals and our nation would heal more quickly. This book closes with questions that the church can ask itself. These questions bring unity and suggest what is necessary for unity to happen. We need to have inclusive conversations with all ethnic groups in order to break down the barriers of our differences. Further, we should explore these misconceptions, misunderstandings, and misinterpretations that exist between us so we can begin to build trust. The world is watching. It all begins with a single step, and the first step should address reconciling our personal relationship with the Lord. This is the goal of Spiritual Formation: that we exchange the yoke of bondage and dismay for Jesus's easy yoke of hope and faithfulness. Then, we can forgive as we open our hearts with compassion to the hearts of each other.

This is where the conversation begins. You see, everyone has a story, and every story is important to God. You now know the thoughts behind the title of this book.

A COMMUNITY JOURNEY, A PERSONAL JOURNEY

Finally, I share my personal reflections throughout this book, revealing the bittersweet awakening of my own inner thoughts, passions, and struggles. I reflect upon the personal revelations of one blinded by unseen strongholds and cultural prejudices. These blind spots in many cases were my protection. On the other hand, they also served as a fortress that clouded and sabotaged my self-perception. Not until I moved beyond these barriers in my time with the Lord was I able to see the need to change my own historical and cultural frames of reference. Then, I could turn toward a healthier and more respectful view of my African heritage and America itself. This has brought about a sense of community and a better understanding of the traditional values that have guided my people's existence. My heart has been stirred, and my commitment to community, as well as my commitment to this nation, is renewed.

For me, just like Sophie of the old story, the little kernels of popcorn over the course of my life journey have opened the eyes of my understanding, restoring my faith that God has been in control of events throughout my life as well as those of my ancestors. More importantly, my journey revives my belief that God is the same yesterday, today, and forever. My prayer is that, by reading this book, you will find restoration for your faith as well.

ONE LET'S TAKE A CLOSER LOOK

Though our story begins with the African slaves' journey to America, everyone has a journey and a story to tell. For many, our ancestral history consists of stories handed down from generation to generation. Let us slow down and take a closer look and see what we can discover.

1. Take some time and revisit your family of origin. What stands out?

2. I wonder what impact our society may be having on you today. Please give this some thought. Write it down.

3. As you were growing up, what were some of your heart's desires?

TWO

Overview of African History and Traditions

> I am because you are, and because you are, therefore I am.
>
> —African Proverb[10]

> Then the LORD God formed man from the dust of the ground, and breathed into his nostrils the breath of life; and the man became a living being.
>
> —GENESIS 2:7, NRSV

IN THE 1900s, after much research and investigation of various African tribes, a new set of authors and researchers developed a more comprehensive view of African heritage and culture than those who had preceded them. For men like John Mbiti, the research revealed that for Africans,

> The whole of [human] existence is a religious phenomenon; man is a deeply religious being living in a religious universe. Failure to realize and appreciate this starting point led missionaries, anthropologists, colonial administrators, and other foreign writers on African religions to see them as pagans or *uncivilized*.

They misunderstand not only the religions as such, but the peoples of African culture.[11]

Fortunately, the study and interaction with various African groups by authors such as John Mbiti, Desmond Tutu, and others have documented these previously misunderstood theological and cultural assumptions about the African belief system.

As we begin to consider the spiritual traditions of the African people, it is important to note that we must not conclude that there were universal beliefs prevalent among all Africans. This is simply not the case. However, the belief systems presented here are representative of a large number of African communities.

EARLY AFRICAN SPIRITUAL BELIEFS AND PRACTICES

The hierarchy of the African belief system begins with the concept of a supreme God. Studies have shown that many concepts deeply embedded within their religious belief systems are concepts also found in Judeo-Christian belief systems. Even without a written language, Africans were able to acknowledge, or have an "acute awareness of something or some other greater than him- or herself."[12] They believed "the universe was created. This presupposes that there was a Creator of the universe.... It seemed to them that the universe must have someone who looks after it, keeps it, sustains it....Man saw how limited his powers and knowledge were particularly in the face of death, calamity, and the forces of nature...which man could not control."[13] They observed, they experienced, and they concluded through their consciences that there existed a higher power above them. Christians view this as God's general revelation to humankind:

> This makes God angry because they have been shown what he is like. Yes, God has made it clear to them. There are things about God that people cannot see—his eternal power and all that makes him God. But since the beginning of the world, those things have been easy for people to understand. They are made clear in what God has made. So people have no excuse for the evil they do.
>
> —ROMANS 1:19-20, ERV

Early African tales reveal that a form of monotheism existed in Africa long before the arrival of the first Europeans. We see this in the oral tradition of stories, proverbs, riddles, myths, and legends handed down from generation to generation. From this, we can gain insight into the culture and behavioral patterns of our African brothers and sisters. Upon close examination, we find that there are several African words used as a description of the Supreme Being. For example, "from the Ashanti people, names of the deity were *Onyuankopon* ('He who alone is great') or *Tetekwaframoa* ('He who endures forever and is of old')."[14] Embodied within these names of a "high God" is an understanding of God's attributes. He is omniscient ("He who knows or sees all" or "He who sees both the inside and the outside of man"). Among the Yoruba people, the Supreme Being was viewed as omnipotent or all-powerful. Thus, they called Him *Olodumare*, meaning "the almighty." The Tonga viewed God as transcendent or "the Limitless One who fills all space."[15]

We see in these names a similarity to the Hebrews' understanding of their relationship with Yahweh, where "the Old Testament psychology is that persons in their totality stand in relation to God and can only be understood in light of this relationship."[16] Likewise, within the African language, we discover little in the way of comprehension as to the nature of God. What we discover is more of the African's response toward God's providence. These oral messages contained within their myths and proverbs communicated not only a means of describing God, but also served to record historical events, warnings of impending danger, and moral teachings.

The African proverb quoted at the beginning of this chapter conveys the conviction that each individual member of society finds the meaning of their existence in relationship with others. Without that relationship, the African has little or no sense of identity. Thus, in African society, individuality is not as important as your membership in a larger community. You are viewed by the community in relation to its laws, traditions, and rituals. Moreover, the success or failure (i.e., survival) of that community hinged upon the conduct and actions of all its members.

It is not until we compare the African ethos of community to certain Western-based concepts of the same that we truly begin to understand the overall significance of community within the African's worldview. Take, for example, the concept of love. Scripture directs us to both love God and "love your neighbor as yourself" (Matthew 22:39b, NRSV). Thus, love is a religious ideal or directive in the Western mindset. Our compulsion to love, if you will, comes from a desire to please God. This is not the case with the African. Morally, Africans bind themselves to duty and commitment to the success of the community. Even though Africans might demonstrate love to others, it is foundational to the culture that, as one prospers, all prosper. In other words, love is viewed less as an ideal or as a religious dictate, and more from the standpoint of being practical for the purpose of survival.

Second, some early Africans did not have a concept of sin that matched the Judeo-Christian concept. God provided the law of the Old Testament to the Israelites and the Great Commandment to New Testament Jews as an internal barometer of the outward expressions of our ability to love and serve Him.

From the African point of view, a transgression or violation of moral conduct committed by an individual was a transgression against the community, not against God. John Mbiti states that in the African community, "Natural calamities are believed to be caused by society…because of its falling moral standards. God brings these calamities to punish the people to bring them back to a proper observance of their morals."[17] To be human from the African perspective was "to belong to the whole community and [to be] involved in its beliefs, ceremonies, rituals, and festivals."[18] Thus, there were consequences to breaking with the community. A person could bring shame upon himself or herself, and that could cause some form of punishment or it could cost a person his or her life. This had a greater significance to them than how a person's actions affect his or her relationship with God.

The last value or ideal to be touched upon is the concept of life after death. Conceptually speaking, the "belief in the continuation of life after death is found in all African societies…but this belief does not constitute a hope for a future and better life. To live here and now is the most important concern of African religious activities and beliefs."[19] There is neither hope for a paradise nor fear of hell in the hereafter. Mbiti states that, unlike Western man, the soul of the African man "does not long for spiritual redemption or for close contact with God in the next world."[20]

Africans placed considerable value on the wisdom of their elders, for it was the conveyance of oral traditions that guided the community in its decision-making. Within the memory banks of the elders were stored the historical recollections of crucial moments in the past that were pertinent to the survival of the tribe and, therefore, the community. They viewed such moments as designed by God, and therefore accepted whatever circumstances resulted from them with dignity. This often resulted in Africans lacking the initiative to move beyond their circumstances.

African people celebrated and observed major events in their lives throughout the community with rituals, ceremonies, and festivals. Occasions warranting such observances by the entire community were "childbirth, the giving of names, circumcision [male and female], marriage, funerals, harvest festivals, praying for rain, etc."[21]

Prayer was a key component of the African community. Traditional prayers included praise, thanksgiving, declaration of the state of affairs, and individual requests. Community-focused prayers petitioned for rain, peace from conflict, cessation of epidemics, a bountiful harvest, and safety from outsiders. As Mbiti observes, prayer helped cultivate the African's dependence on God, thereby increasing his spiritual outreach.[22] These prayers were often accompanied by sacrifices using the "blood of human beings, animals, or birds; offerings involved the giving of other things, such as foodstuffs, water, milk, or money."[23]

It is worth pausing here to examine the contrast between an African view of Spiritual Formation and the view of Spiritual Formation held by the majority of modern American Christians.

From a strictly Eurocentric view, Spiritual Formation and soul care are the spiritual disciplines whose goal is the transformation of the *individual* Christian believer into the image and likeness of Christ. These disciplines can include prayer/meditation, praise, and worship. Similar disciplines exist in the lifestyles of the indigenous African people; however, such religious traditions and culture exist through the larger lens of community and their *combined* relationship with a "higher power." Alternatively, in twenty-first century America, spiritual disciplines are a means of nurture, meant to open one's heart to the Lord.

For the early Africans, these disciplines were a fundamental way of life, handed down through the centuries from one generation to the next. Modes of expression included music, singing, and dance, and we find that they encompassed every level of human activity from birth, to marriage, to family, to death, and, finally, to the afterlife. Since each tribe observed its own communal infrastructure, we find that religious observances contributed highly to one's sense of identity within their community, thereby helping to establish a sense of pride and dignity of their own community, as distinct from neighboring tribes.

The tribes were unique entities unto themselves, often lacking any relational dynamics with other tribes. This sense of communal pride and dignity led to strong social support systems within each community. The impetus for helping those in need was not based upon any sense of a "higher calling," as is observed in most Western cultures, but rather from the basis of community need and survival. Therefore, an assumption could be that an African loved his neighbor only in the sense that he viewed that neighbor through the lens of the larger community to which they both belonged.

Later in the book, we will return to the subject of Spiritual Formation, keeping this Western/African contrast in mind (see chapter 6).

PRE-COLONIAL AFRICA AND SLAVERY

When conducting an overview of culture in pre-Colonial Africa, we must not forget that slave labor was a widespread cultural norm from biblical times forward. In fact, historically speaking, it was only rather recently that conquering armies stopped considering enemy prisoners as spoils of war. Since this custom was common in Africa, we must assume that most African tribes ultimately impacted by the transatlantic slave trade were well acquainted with the practice of slavery long before the arrival of the first European.

POST-COLONIAL SLAVE TRADE

With the advent of Colonialism, improved communication, and new trade routes, the need for commodities and services between countries such as Turkey and China increased. Available resources for slave labor began to dwindle, especially among the Turkish and Muslim countries. These countries were no longer an adequate source of labor for the Portuguese. Out of this necessity, the Portuguese (among the preeminent

Regions for the Transatlantic Slave Trade

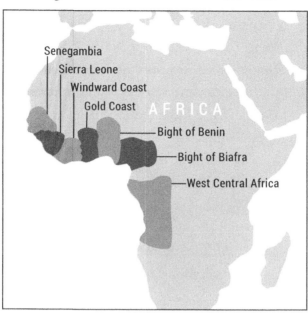

mariners of the fourteenth and fifteenth centuries) eventually turned toward the African continent as an untapped resource of slave labor. See the regions for the transatlantic slave trade on the map above.

African slaves harvested sugar on the coast of Guinea, and farmed and mined in the countries of Cuba and Hispaniola. The need for African slaves increased and quickly spread to Brazil, the Caribbean, and the southern portion of what is today the United States.

Slavery, "the state or condition of being held in involuntary servitude as the property of somebody else,"[24] began to flourish among territories colonized by Western Europeans as the result of a decree issued by Pope Nicholas V in 1452. In this

decree, the pope granted Afonso V of Portugal the right to re-
duce any "Saracens, pagans, and any other unbelievers" to he-
reditary slavery (this decree was later reaffirmed and extended
through another papal "bull," issued in 1455). Together, these
decrees not only served to justify the subsequent era of slave
trade, but they also came to serve as a "means to embark on a
holy war for the defense and increase of religion as a model for
future European conquests."[25]

The king of Portugal took full advantage of this edict
to enslave "pagan" Africans and to expand trade between the
new world and Western Europe. Caught in a web of greed and
politics orchestrated by people with whom they had no relations whatsoever, Africans from multiple cultures—men and
women who were everything from royalty to warriors, from
priests to agricultural farmers—were stripped of their dignity
and reduced to mere chattel or a commodity. Exiting through
the "Door of No Return,"[26] they boarded slave ships *en route*
through the middle passage of the transatlantic trade route to
the Americas.

In addition to those trafficked to the Americas, other
workers were sold as indentured servants to outlying European and Asian countries; however, these Africans were afforded
the opportunity to marry, build families, and acquire land—a
much different fate than those who found themselves sold to
plantation owners in the Southern United States.

Centuries ago, God laid the foundational groundwork
for the knowledge of God's existence in the hearts of the
African people. This would pave the way to their acceptance
of God and God's Son, Jesus. In retrospect, however, we

see that "the Western psychology of self…influenced by Descartes' dictum, 'I think, therefore I am'"[27] has subtly drawn African-Americans away from the original value system of community—a system that brought unity and harmony.

What is the remedy when the African-American's naturalistic tendency for community comes into conflict with the Eurocentric worldview toward individualism? Even more so, how can we obtain a clear understanding of what African-Americans have suffered at the hands of this redefining paradigm? These questions draw attention to the inner struggle of African-Americans in this nation—a struggle that we will examine from the perspective of both culture and history in the next few chapters.

TWO LET'S TAKE A CLOSER LOOK

This section describes our cultural history beginning with our roots in Africa. Today, many use Ancestry.com and other sources to search the history of their families. Documented or undocumented, family traits are passed down from generation to generation.

1. How has your identity been shaped by family history and traditions?

2. What moments of your story do you cherish?

3. The early slaves used music to soothe and endure the pains of slavery. Describe your haven for retreat and solace in difficult times.

THREE

The Spiritual Journey to Freedom

> The Spirit of the Lord is upon me, because he has anointed me to bring good news to the poor. He has sent me to proclaim release to the captives and recovery of sight to the blind, to let the oppressed go free, to proclaim the year of the Lord's favor.
>
> —LUKE 4:18-19, NRSV

> Your boasting is not a good thing. Do you not know that a little yeast leavens the whole batch of dough?
>
> —1 CORINTHIANS 5:6, NRSV

THE SPARSELY POPULATED, agriculture-based colonies of what later became the American South suffered under economic hardships not experienced by their Northern neighbors. They lacked enough inexpensive labor to cultivate properly the rich, fertile farmlands of Virginia, the Carolinas, Georgia, Alabama, and Mississippi. In the North, agriculture developed on a smaller scale: farms tended to remain at a size manageable by a single farmer and his family. This was not the case in the South, where weather and acreage were more suitable to the production of crops on a large scale. Thus, the Southern colonies lagged behind their Northern neighbors both economically and in population. From the Southern perspective, the obvious solution to the problem was to import cheap labor, and the cheapest, most economic, most effective labor available to colonists in the Western Hemisphere was from Africa.

As the American colonies took hold and began to grow, African and African-American slaves soon replaced Caucasians and Native Americans as the primary source of labor on newly developed farmlands, especially in the South. The map on page 41 reflects the slave trade routes. In fact, between 1450 and 1900, almost 500,000 Africans were imported to North America, with some 350,000 to 400,000 arriving on the eastern shores of the United States. The table on page 41 contains the transatlantic imports by region.

A numeric statistical view of slave imports provides a clearer picture of exploitation with over 10 million Africans stripped of their homeland and transported to another country and culture. See the distribution of slaves by census chart on page 42. Still, we are not the only nationality that faced such horrific treatment.

ECONOMICS OF THE NORTH AND SOUTH

In the North, Puritan and Quaker settlers (both persecuted in England) arrived on the Atlantic seaboard in search of religious freedom. Over time, the Puritans, whose religious beliefs did not permit the promotion of slavery, twisted their theological doctrines to justify domination of both Native Americans and African slaves, thus propagating the belief that both groups were inferior to White Europeans. The Quakers, who doctrinally were proponents of peace and racial equality, opposed war and

Triangular Slave Trade Routes

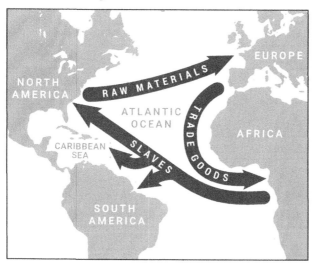

Transatlantic Imports by Region 1450-1900[28]

Region	Number of Slaves Accounted For	Percent Per Region
Brazil	4,000,000	35.4%
Spanish Empire	2,500,000	22.1%
British West Indies	2,000,000	17.7%
French West Indies	1,600,000	14.1%
British, North America, and United States	500,000	4.4%
Dutch West Indies	500,000	4.4%
Danish West Indies	28,000	0.2%
Europe (and Islands)	200,000	1.8%
Total	11,328,000	100%

Distribution of Slaves by Census

Census Year	Number of Slaves	Number of Free Blacks	Total Blacks	Percent of Free Blacks	Total US Population	Percent Blacks of Total
1790	697,681	59,527	757,208	7.9%	3,929,214	19%
1800	893,602	108,435	1,002,037	10.8%	5,308,483	19%
1810	1,191,362	186,446	1,377,808	13.5%	7,239,881	19%
1820	1,538,022	233,634	1,771,656	13.2%	9,638,453	18%
1830	2,009,043	319,599	2,328,642	13.7%	12,860,702	18%
1840	2,487,355	386,293	2,873,648	13.4%	17,063,353	17%
1850	3,204,313	434,495	3,638,808	11.9%	23,191,876	16%
1860	3,953,760	488,070	4,441,830	11%	31,443,321	14%
1870	0	4,880,009	4,880,009	100%	38,558,371	13%

Source: https://census.gov/content/dam/Census/library/working-papers/2002/demo/POP-twps0056.pdf

slavery, but still denied free Blacks the opportunity to assimilate and integrate into their communities.

As Paul R. Griffin observes, "Domination and degradation of black people was not a mere economic or social necessity. Racial supremacy was a divine mandate that Whites had to constantly practice, lest they violate their covenant with God."[29] From the Calvinist point of view, slavery of Black Africans "drew a vision of God at work providentially in the lives of black people, directing their sufferings yet promising the faithful among them a restoration to his favor and his presence."[30] In other words, many Whites believed themselves divinely appointed as overseers of the Black Africans and that any attempt to overthrow slavery was contrary to God's will. Even in cases where White Christians of the time opposed the practice of slavery, many, like the Quakers, remained unprepared to accept Black people as their equals.

For obvious reasons, White Christians promulgated similar theological views in the South. Some White Christians attempted to proselytize slaves to the Christian faith by teaching them how to read, using the Bible as the primary source of reading material. Educating the Africans in this manner was an accepted practice, until it became evident that God's Word aligned itself perfectly with the Africans' desire for freedom. This eventually led to the unfortunate result of intermittent slave revolts of which Nat Turner's revolt (August 1831) is prominent.

As Gayraud Wilmore notes, "The role of religion in fomenting and guiding insurrections must give considerable credit to the fact that radical white Christians taught the Negroes how to read the Bible in such a way as to discover the relevance of their faith to the quest of liberation."[31]

These slave insurrections triggered the White Southern population to enact literacy laws and various pieces of local legislation designed to dismantle the psyches of the slaves by restricting their movements and preventing them from learning to read altogether.

According to Na'im Akbar, we must keep in mind that "the process of human slavery is ultimately a psychological process by which the mind of a people is gradually brought under the control of their captors and they become imprisoned by the loss of the consciousness (awareness) of themselves."[32] Thus, the slave owner saw nothing wrong with distorting Scripture or enacting laws that prohibited the education of slaves, as long as those actions served to squash thoughts of freedom among Blacks.

Akbar continues, "The goal was to dismantle any and all mechanisms that preserved the continuity of the African people."[33] White slaveholders used books, laws,[34] training manuals, slave trainers, religion, and the misinterpretation of biblical allegory (i.e., "curse of Ham") to justify the slave owners' inhumane treatment of their slaves. We find this borne out in an excerpt of a presentation made by Willie Lynch, a British West Indies plantation owner. His speech chronicled the method he used to break down the African psyche and pit each slave against the other:

> We reversed nature by burning and pulling a civilized n----- apart and bull whipping the other to the point of death, all in her [*the African mother*] presence. By her being left alone, unprotected, and the male image destroyed, the ordeal caused her to move from her psychologically dependent state to a frozen, independent state. In this frozen, psychological state of independence, she will raise her male and female offspring in reversed roles. For fear of the young male's life, she will psychologically train him to be mentally weak and dependent, but physically strong. Because she has become psychologically independent, she will train her female off spring's [sic] to be psychological independent. What have you got? You've got the n----- woman out front and the n----- man behind and scared.[35]

Another tactic used by Southern plantation owners was to engage trained Black preachers from the North to preach a "rally call to obedience" among their slaves, thereby reinforcing the theology that Whites were superior to Blacks. This had the obvious effect of diminishing the White man's theology in the minds of the slaves. As Mitchell has observed, "The message to them [the slaves] was to obey the 'massa', which made the white religion without credulity."[36]

Yet these same Black preachers, at great risk to their own lives, attended secret nightly meetings where they taught the slaves the true biblical message, assuring them that God did love them, and that they were His children. "You are created in God's image. You are not slaves; you are not n-----s; you are God's children."[37]

Upon hearing these polarized messages, it is understandable how the theology of slaves became somewhat skewed. Add to this the fact that the slaves had to learn a new language, without any teachers, and that they had limited exposure to Christian ideals or corporate worship. One wonders how the Gospel message was able to penetrate their community at all. Yet penetrate it did. Slaves used "praise houses" (unused buildings where they were allowed to meet), brush arbors, or just hollowed-out places and forest clearings for times of prayer, worship meetings, ring shouts, and community fellowship. Though heavily influenced by White Christianity, they retained their own style of worship. Mitchell describes it this way: "To keep the heat off, they smiled and showed themselves submissive during the day, while at night they gathered with their pots and cried out to the Lord."[38] By crying into the pot, they reduced the noise level of the prayer gatherings and minimized their chances of discovery by their disapproving overseers. More important are the prayers spoken into those pots. They were prayers of freedom for themselves and freedom for the generations to come.

JOURNEY TO FREEDOM

Yes, the common concept of a "high God," a concept that found its roots in Africa, unfolded in the Americas. The slaves saw God as the "most high," transcendent, and the Creator of heaven and earth, yet unreachable. My inner soul laments over the cruelty of their overseers and masters who claimed to be Christians. Unable to reconcile their masters' actions and behaviors with Christianity (and unable, because of cruel anti-literacy laws, to check the slave owners' theology against Scripture itself), many withdrew and conversion was made difficult. Others were able to identify more with the biblical narratives about Jesus helping others. For them, Jesus would be a lesser god, in accordance with their African belief system. This Jesus visited His people and was concerned with their daily life and life in the community. He was a suffering servant, a doer of good, crucified unjustly. Other biblical stories of deliverance also captured the Africans' attention. They learned of the great exodus from Egypt, or the plight of the three Hebrew boys (Shadrach, Meshach, and Abednego),[39] or simply the story of Daniel in the lions' den. The death of an innocent man on the cross, Jesus, who tried to help others and died for the sins of all, spurred hope of freedom and deliverance. Here, "it is important to remember also that no single African culture or religion, once transplanted in alien soil, could have remained intact."[40]

In time, church preaching would influence the rich heritage of the slaves' religious beliefs. Regardless, the stories of the biblical narrative touched the slaves' souls. If God could deliver these, surely He could deliver them. The God that was far away had drawn nearer to their hearts through God's Son, and this "presence" manifested in the daily routine of the enslaved. "Religion permeated every dimension of African life during slavery. They carried their spirituality everywhere, refusing to separate the supernatural from the natural, and the sacred from the secular."[41]

AFRICAN TRADITIONAL INFLUENCES

Through these stories, God continued to engage the hearts of those enslaved in the South, and an ever-increasing percentage surrendered their hearts to this previously unknown or, at least, unrecognized Deity. Yet at the same time, we find evidence that they maintained at least two very important traditions from their African heritage. The first was the well-entrenched tradition of community. In the midst of toil, torture, and injustice, they were more concerned about solidarity as a community of sufferers than they were about fear or about the consequences from their master's whip. "They wondered not whether God was just and right but whether the sadness and pain of this world would cause them to lose faith in the Gospel of God."[42]

It was out of this environment that the enslaved Africans drew upon another of their ancient traditions that had been a vital element of their tribal system for countless generations: "the song." The songs they sang as an enslaved community were quite different from those they sang in their native lands. These new songs were not the chant-and-rhythm melodies of the motherland. Instead, the songs they sang as slaves derived from the physical abuse and inner turmoil they suffered on a daily basis. Uniquely birthed from within the slave community, the songs that became more commonly known as "Negro spirituals" transitioned "between hope and despair, joy and sorrow, death and life."[43] They became opportunities for slaves to have an encounter with the God who would bring them both salvation and freedom. Consequently, it was out of a seemingly hopeless situation "where human life is regarded as property and death has no dignity...[that] the slaves found ways to hold together their personhood."[44]

The following lines of a well-known spiritual lament depict a wounded heart finding a shared hope in community with others:

> *Nobody knows de trouble I see,*
> *Nobody knows but Jesus*
> *Nobody knows de trouble I see*
> *Glory, hallelujah!*[45]

It was not until they arrived in the United States that the Africans learned of the Christian concept of an afterlife. Thus, even in the midst of their suffering were thoughts of a future hope and a trust that the God of all justice would vindicate them.

> *Swing low, sweet chariot,*
> *Coming for to carry me home*
> *Swing low, sweet chariot,*
> *Coming for to carry me home.*
>
> *I looked over Jordan, and what did I see*
> *Coming for to carry me home?*
> *A band of angels coming after me*
> *Coming for to carry me home.*[46]

Of course, the concept of "home" in this particular spiritual could easily have a double meaning. To many slaves, home was Africa herself, or at the very least, Africa was the place where they had once enjoyed strong bonds of community. For those who became followers of Jesus, home for them was the life to come, that place where all suffering would cease forever.

As previously observed, Africans had no concept of an afterlife, and certainly no concept of eternal suffering. Divine justice was in the context of daily events and outcomes. However, with the introduction of Judeo-Christian theology into the slave culture, they began to view that the teaching of an "afterlife of fire and brimstone only dramatized in new detail the implementation of a divine justice known and trusted in Africa."[47]

Through their increased understanding of our Lord, the slaves readily embraced Jesus's trial and struggle, reproducing His struggle in song and articulating their desire to be with Him. So they sang, and when they sang, they sang together in community, as they had in the motherland. Sometimes, the deep-felt emotion brought dancing, sometimes crying, yet still they sang. These emotional expressions were not due entirely to their daily hardships. Cone believes, "The physical brutalities of slavery were minor in comparison to the loss of the community."[48] This point is of great significance because any present-day attempt at unity and reconciliation within our culture and among our cultures must address not only the individual sense of loss or suffering, but also the loss of community as experienced by African-Americans. These two issues intertwine but are not the same. Yes, the slave experienced brutalities that left scars still evident today. That same slave experienced a second loss: the loss of the community safety net that had undergirded his entire cultural experience in Africa.

Repeatedly, we see this hunger for "home" reflected in the Negro spirituals. For the slave, suffering from the pangs of separation, "going home" was more than a mere expectation of relief or escapism. It was "an affirmation of the need for community. It was the place where mother, father, sister, and brother had gone."[49]

> *Sometimes I feel like a motherless child*
> *Sometimes I feel like a motherless child*
> *Sometimes I feel like a motherless child*
> *A long ways from home*
> *A long ways from home*[50]

Out of their newfound faith in God's providence, the enslaved had confidence that a returning Jesus would take them to a new home in heaven. So they would sing:

> *I got shoes; you got shoes all o' God's chillun got shoes*
> *When I get to heab'n I'm goin' to put on my shoes*
> *I'm goin' to walk all over God's Heab'n Heab'n Heab'n*[51]

Then, because they expected God to punish those who enslaved them, they would look over their shoulders toward the plantation house (or, as the slaves would say, the "Big House") and sing:

> *Ev'rybody talkin' bout Heab'n ain't goin' dere*
> *Heab'n Heab'n*[52]

The lyrics return to the reflection of their own future inheritance as they continued:

I'm goin' to walk all ovah God's Heab'n
I got a robe, you got a robe o' God's chillun got a robe
When I get to heab'n I'm goin' to put on my robe
I'm goin' to shout all ovah God's Heab'n Heab'n Heab'n [53]

We find this same message hidden in other songs as well:

Steal away, steal away, steal away to Jesus
Steal away, steal away home
I ain't got long to stay here [54]

As we pursue a course that leads toward forgiveness and racial reconciliation, it is important for all to recognize how these subtle yet profound expressions of both pain and hope affect life. Just as I have noted in this brief introduction to a bit of the slave history, every culture and every generation should share and remember their historical story. For African-Americans, the "Negro spiritual" is core to our survival and an important part of our journey. Through these songs, we begin to recognize the suffering that drove the enslaved to a state of desolation. Yet, as Kellemen and Edwards note, "The slave spirituals also bred hope, granting others permission to join in the struggle. It was in the language of these spirituals that other slaves began to communicate of their own pain…of their despair. [55]

No more weeping and a-wailing
No more weeping and a-wailing
No more weeping and a-wailing
I'm goin' to live with God [56]

Many of the songs sung by slaves looked past struggles of daily life toward the anticipation of a heavenly realm. Thus, they would sing:

I want t' meet my Jesus
I want t' meet my Jesus
I want t' meet my Jesus
I'm goin' to live with God[57]

or

Soon-a will be done a-with the troubles of the world
Troubles of the world, troubles of the world,
Soon-a will be done a-with the troubles of the world
Goin' home to live with God[58]

With the understanding that death would end their physical suffering, the songs of the enslaved spoke to both consolation for the present and an everlasting promise for the future:

I've been 'buked an' I've been scorned, children
I've been 'buked an' I've been scorned
I've been talked about, sho's you're born

Dere is trouble all over dis world
Children, dere is trouble all over dis world

Ain't gwine to lay my 'ligion down[59]
Children, ain't gwine to lay my 'ligion down

Singing is a mainstay in African-American churches today, and worship is the outward expression of the love and need for the Lord that ministers to the inward pain of our experiences. Similarly, the slaves sang together and consoled each other in community.

In the South after the Civil War, though many mourned their losses, God had provided havens of consolation where the freed slaves could tell their stories. Octavia Albert, a pastor's wife, writer, and spiritual guide, provided one such haven by opening her home to freed slaves. Initially, her goal was to publish writings that would correct our history and track the progress of ex-slaves; however, the Lord also used her as a spiritual guide and friend. Her home became a respite to those who sought rest from this weary journey. She interviewed and provided consolation for numerous ex-slaves, such as Charlotte Brooks, who had lost her parents and all her children and said, "Gone, and no one to care for me."[60] Even then, there were sanctuaries for self-care, where those present heard the woes of the human heart. Mrs. Albert's home was a place where Charlotte would return often.

One could view this as a place of retreat: a place that valued prayer, meditation, and solitude. On the plantation, the enslaved practiced these spiritual disciplines when they were in bondage, though they looked different then; the slaves would retreat to the forest and quiet places, or use their pots to cry out to their Lord.

Upon reflection, we can see how they experienced intimacy with the Lord and how He was with them. Charlotte had a place to go and a spiritual friend or guide welcoming her. As believers, we must not overlook the importance of this invitation from the Lord—"Come to Me"—an invitation to come to an environment where we feel safe, where the soft, concerned, compassionate, and empathetic voice of a spiritual friend or guide listens to the heartbeat of the inner Spirit and prays. For African-Americans, during this time the basic spiritual practices were not available. It did not matter, for God uniquely used those like Mrs. Albert to care for the souls of His people, especially those who had a full understanding of their own heart's lament—even if they were devoid of the experience of a formal language and formal education. How can one doubt the power of the Holy Spirit of truth who uniquely, without necessarily using a formal form or fashion, draws humankind to Himself?

Even with broken or incomplete religious teaching, the unlearned slaves were able to look past the fallibility of doctrinal error to see truth and survive. They endured the painful schemes of the oppressors and the religious instruction of a mangled Gospel designed with an eye toward psychological destruction, but those undertakings did not destroy their zeal for future freedom.

Nonetheless, these inner scars did not go away; they had an impact on the slave's ability to trust man, even those within their own ranks. Through years of loss and mistreatment, while they were dehumanized, disfigured, disgraced, and disenfranchised, the enslaved continued to live in community and in hope. "The oppressor would discover that the downtrodden cannot be destroyed forever, because God forever stands against those who exercise…mastery over the least of his children."[61] They never stopped singing, they never stopped praying, they never stopped praising, and they never stopped hoping. These songs are a reminder to African-Americans today of their solidarity.

In time, the solidarity of the slaves would prove to be an obstacle in the unifying efforts of freedmen in post–Civil War times. The culture subjected freedmen to a divided social ethic, a divided church, and a strained governmental system that would handicap the unifying efforts of the freed people in a nation scarred from war. Chapter 4 will address some of the factors that hindered our inclusion in the birth of a nation.

These three paradigm shifts are still issues that African-Americans fight today. Back then, societal impacts in the North and South were different. Rebuilding the South would be painstakingly difficult. The Reconstruction Era did not produce the desired results. Eventually, Congress recalled the federal troops, who enforced the laws to ensure another uprising did not occur. The focus of the Southern population, many of whom had lost everything, was on reestablishing their lives. In addition, desolated families suffering from homelessness, poverty, and hunger were trying to rebuild and had little empathy for the freedmen's plight. Governmental intentions of inclusion for the newly freed population did not change the belief system of many Southerners and only highlighted the inferiority of the Blacks and the superiority of the Whites. Finally, schisms in the church over slavery were ongoing. In the North, the freed Blacks were trying to establish their own centers of worship, while conversions for those in the South became difficult because the Black population could not read.

SEEDS OF HOPE

It is important to note that not all Whites condoned the slavery system. There were those who were sympathetic to the plight of the enslaved Africans, and these "sympathizers" became instruments of the Lord, serving an important role by keeping the slavery issue before the public.

In spite of the law, some liberal White sympathizers taught African slaves to read. Using the Bible as their text, these "missionaries" to the slaves were responsible for proclaiming God's good news to the Africans. Abolitionist groups, like the Society of Friends (i.e., the Quakers), held protests, published pamphlets, and worked with the Underground Railroad— some alongside Harriet Tubman, an escaped slave. The American Colonization Society, which was organized in 1817, raised money to remunerate masters for their slaves so that they could send these former slaves back to Africa (Liberia). Other sympathizers who served in the abolitionist movement volunteered through local church associations. Newspaper publications such as *The North Star*, established and written by Frederick Douglass, and *The Liberator*, edited by William Lloyd Garrison, kept the issue of slavery before the colonial people. The fervor of this movement also manifested itself through protests and marches.

Unfortunately, other more diabolical fields of study emerged as well. "While both southern and northern preachers and trained theologians were proclaiming a God-ordained black inferiority, scientists such as the renowned Jean-Louis Agassiz...connected scientific theories to the theological ones...to infer that black people are innately inferior to whites and that...white people must dominate black people because they are 'naturally' incapable of high civilization."[62] These racist ideas raised the question, Are African-Americans still "bred to be led"?[63]

As we can see, America was divided, and not solely on the institution of slavery. The division was affecting public life both socially and theologically, and along racial lines as well. This fact did not change with the end of the Civil War.

This divide created an enormous obstacle in the efforts to unify North and South, and particularly Blacks and Whites, in post–Civil War America. Thus, inroads toward forgiveness and reconciliation were virtually impossible.

And Sophie continues to drop kernels of popcorn.

THREE LET'S TAKE A CLOSER LOOK

The story of slavery is not the only story. There are stories within our family, stories in our neighborhood, stories from our job, and stories in our relationships. All play a role in shaping our value systems and self-worth. We do know this—the Lord loves us and cares about all our stories.

1. Let's take a look back. What have you noticed about your culture of origin?

2. Describe the safeguards that you put in place to protect your heart. What did you observe?

3. Look back again. What would you do differently? How would you raise your family differently?

4. In your life's journey, what have you discerned of the historical past that continues to be an imprint on your life and your decisions?

FOUR

Post–Civil War Overview

> Come to me, all you that are weary and are carrying heavy
> burdens, and I will give you rest. Take my yoke upon you,
> and learn from me; for I am gentle and humble in heart,
> and you will find rest for your souls. For my yoke is easy,
> and my burden is light.
>
> —MATTHEW 11:28-30, NRSV

> Life, Liberty and the pursuit of Happiness.
>
> —THE DECLARATION OF INDEPENDENCE

PRESIDENT LINCOLN'S GOAL was to reunite a divided
country and bring together disparate factions that were battling
over a state's right to enslave human beings for economic
purposes. The issue had literally torn our nation apart, resulting
in a great civil conflict that was having devastating results
on both sides. Lincoln's hope (maybe even his prayer) was
that the two sides would again become one, that the United
States would truly become a nation of equality for all men.
Unfortunately, that dream has failed to become a reality, even
to this day. John Wilkes Booth assassinated President Lincoln
on April 15, 1865.

A new president took the helm: Andrew Johnson, whose interests and beliefs were contrary to his predecessor. Charged with the responsibility of rebuilding the South and extending civil rights and suffrage to former slaves, President Johnson soon made it apparent that he would not use his presidential influence to engage the Southern states or be proactive in the reconstruction efforts. Unlike President Lincoln, President Johnson believed slavery to be a necessity for the South. He issued pardons and amnesty to any Confederates and high-ranking officers who would take an oath of allegiance. Outraged by his performance, Congress passed the Freedmen's Bureau Act[64] and the Civil Rights Act of 1866.[65] While in office, President Johnson did not reshape the thinking of the post-war American citizen and did not bring unity to the nation. By 1868, President Johnson lost his credibility; he brought disgrace and ridicule upon Congress and faced impeachment. Though the impeachment attempt was unsuccessful, President Johnson's beliefs remained unchanged as Congress continued to override his veto of reconstruction bills until the end of his term in office.

What this nation became, however, was a collection of people groups experiencing vastly different realities within the same society. Instead of melding into a single people with a common understanding of history and religion, we became a nation with differing points of view concerning our own history and concerning God. Even our perception of Scripture varied depending on the color of our skin. As time passed, this resulted in our collective inability to comprehend the depth and breadth of racial tensions in our populace. For White Americans, this disparity in understanding may have brought about a sense of gratification and even entitlement, while Black Americans were left feeling marginalized and excluded, having experienced poverty, injustice, and a loss of dignity. Freedom for all culminated in African-Americans being forsaken and unable to integrate into the "land of the free and the home of the brave."

In post–Civil War America, this duality proved to be a dilemma as a divided population set about rebuilding the country. No one had realized the magnitude of this undertaking or projected what would become of ex-slaves in the rebuilding process. Even supporters of the anti-slavery movement were not mentally prepared to embrace and integrate newly freed people of color.

THE ERA OF RECONSTRUCTION

Though slavery was at an end, racism and systemic oppression of Black people were not. During Reconstruction, the Black codes, Jim Crow laws, and lynch mobs in both the North and South replaced the formal institutions of slavery, rendering most of the nation's Blacks second-class citizens, at best. The term used in the twenty-first century is "racial profiling."

With so many unresolved national issues, the American government was unable to process the humanitarian themes associated with racial inequality. Moreover, the church, which had historically served as the social "safety net" throughout U.S. history, was itself dealing with division and, therefore, was unable to fully unite and come to the aid of the returning Northern and Southern soldiers from the war, including the freed Blacks. Finally, only complicating the drama, our nation was encountering a flood of new immigrants from Western Europe, all of whom were seeking a new life and the means to survive. The U.S. Congress faced large-scale issues surrounding urban poverty, mass unemployment, social justice, and mental health. These social issues took precedence over racial equality for Black Americans and other people groups facing similar challenges.

With the advent of Reconstruction, the Confederacy ended, and approximately 4 million slaves gained their freedom. Congress went to work rebuilding a nation torn apart by war, taking steps along the way to amend the Constitution with the passing of the Thirteenth Amendment, which abolished slavery. In 1868, the Fourteenth Amendment provided for the equal treatment of all citizens, regardless of race, and the Fifteenth Amendment extended the right to vote to all citizens regardless of race. Additional federal legislation addressed the ability of all citizens to participate equally in government, which aided Black Americans in gaining an equal footing in society and the economy. Legally, Blacks could now own land, vote, and hold political office.

The Southern states rejoined the Union, ratifying new state constitutions in the process. Economic advancements in the South included the educational system, railroads, housing, and hospitals. Industry advanced as steel, cotton, and lumber mills reinvigorated the economy in the South.

Charitable organizations and concerned citizens, both Black and White, worked to improve education and literacy among Black Americans. Various Black institutions gained momentum, and African-American churches succeeded in

gaining their independence from predominantly White denominations. Notwithstanding these advances, many Southern Blacks remained isolated within their communities, unable
to trust the intentions of outsiders. Blacks as a whole began
building new lives, while others became sharecroppers, which
meant working under conditions very similar to those they had
worked under as slaves. These sharecroppers suffered abject
poverty at the hands of corrupt landowners and carpetbaggers.

In time, the positive impacts of Reconstruction would
fade. Rebuilding from the devastation caused by the Civil War
proved too costly. Congressional interest lost its impetus, and
the lack of solidarity would prove to be a deterrent in efforts to
unify the South and to assimilate Black Americans into society.

As we close out our look at the era of Reconstruction, we
see that the United States had changed. The country witnessed
its first presidential impeachment—that of Andrew Johnson. In
the midst of congressional turmoil, opportunities were opening
up for immigrants to build homes for their families in the new
territories westward. New industries were on the horizon, and
the country was on the move and growing. Nonetheless, not
all was well. Three great divides still plagued American culture.

The first division was economic. In the aftermath of the
war, many White families suffered from homelessness, poverty,
and hunger. In their efforts to reestablish themselves, they had
little empathy for the plight of Black Americans. As can be
seen, without a combined integrated effort toward rebuilding
the South, the impact of the Freedmen's Bureau and similar
programs was drastically reduced, prohibiting Blacks from
gaining a true economic foothold.

A second divide that negatively affected the freed slave was the schism between churches in the North and churches in the South. The church chose compromise over union. Notwithstanding either the war's outcome or amendments to our federal Constitution, the issue of slavery remained unsettled in the minds and hearts of many. In the North, where the stigma against racial integration was not as severe, this theological divide caused freed Blacks to establish their own centers of worship. In the pro-slavery South, where social disapproval against integration ran high, the message of the church remained unchanged: "Blacks were made to be slaves." Enraged, many freed Blacks flocked to independent Black churches or built their own worship centers. Eventually, Americans learned to worship separately from one another.

A third divide greatly affecting post–Civil War Reconstruction was a strained governmental system ill equipped to handle the enormous financial and labor costs associated with the efforts to reunify our nation. Because of this weakness, many Southerners rejected efforts put forth by the federal government toward reconstruction, believing the administrative oversight of the local or state government to be more suitable to recovery undertakings. In addition, the ventures of private, self-seeking carpetbaggers and other opportunists were instrumental in stunting economic opportunities and prosperity in the Southern states. Unfortunately, their actions often culminated in violence, and the progress of the freed Blacks stalemated. These various conditions all contributed to the spiritual weakening of our overall society, eventually leading to the emergence of the Ku Klux Klan and other White supremacist groups.

While separated from these events by almost 150 years, we still experience the vestiges of these three divides today. Even though African-Americans continue to feel isolated from mainstream society, strong family ties remain the strength of the Black family. Through affirmations within our family structure, we have become educated and built thriving businesses. We have become creative inventors, are steadfast in the entertainment industry, and have shaped strategies for economic development. Many of our communities have prospered. We also serve and continue to serve in the commercial arena, as civil servants and as political arms in local, state, and national governments to secure this nation as a world force.

THE AFRICAN-AMERICAN RELIGIOUS MOVEMENT

The spiritual journey of African-Americans began pre–Civil War on the plantation. White missionaries and African-American preachers, whether they were hired by the slave owner or were working alongside their brothers and sisters in the fields, secretly shared the Gospel of love message—often at great personal risk—with Southern slaves.

The Second Great Awakening (1795–1835) sowed seeds of revival throughout the nation. These religious meetings were multi-denominational and responsible for the conversion of many American-born Blacks, most of whom funneled into existing Methodist and Baptist churches. This was not only the first experience in a traditional church setting for the newly "born-again" Black Americans, it was also among the first examples of integrating what had previously been an exclusively White institution.

As memberships of these mixed congregations grew, new challenges surfaced. White church members were uncomfortable with a mixed worship experience, especially with the outward expression of emotions by African-Americans. Racist attitudes concerning the lay representation and governance by Blacks in the church caused conflicts. Women were not exempt from these racist attitudes. The church prohibited women from serving in church governance or pursuing major leadership roles. Still today, women fight to have a voice in many congregations and denominations. Finally, the church's core beliefs were under scrutiny. As Dr. Henry Mitchell has observed, "Once white Methodists and Baptists ceased to need African-American support to get congregations started and sanctuaries built, and once they began their upward climb from a lower-class fringe movement to respectability, they wanted the socio-ethnic lines clearly drawn."[66] Dr. Mitchell contends that "deep down, the issue surrounded class, culture, and control"[67] and not love.

Given the African-American's desire to maintain certain cultural rituals and traditions from Africa, a split was no doubt inevitable. However, there was no set process for Black church members to establish their own church. Mitchell notes that "no church, North or South, evolved without some form of white denominational recognition, trusteeship of land title, and/or certification to the government by respected whites that the blacks involved would cause...no trouble."[68] In time, Whites lifted these restraints, and the Black congregants would form independent Black churches with their own governing bodies.

GROWTH OF THE AFRICAN-AMERICAN CHURCH IN THE NORTH

To understand the growth of African-American churches in the North after the Civil War, we must understand the history of the African-American church in the North *before* the Civil War.

At the conclusion of the Revolutionary War (1783), some slave owners, like the Quakers, either freed their slaves or offered them the opportunity to purchase their freedom, so the overall Black church population grew.

Even though there were a few sizeable Black congregations in the Northern states, it was not until 1795 that the Episcopal Church ordained its first African-American deacon, Absalom Jones, who in 1802 became the first ordained Black Episcopal priest of the African Episcopal Church of St. Thomas in Philadelphia. The same was true of the Methodist Episcopal Church. After years of subjection to discrimination at the hands of White leadership, African-Americans formed the first independent Black denomination (African Methodist Episcopal) in 1816, naming Richard Allen our nation's first Black bishop. Elevation to this position did not impede his passion to serve God's people or his passion for freedom. In the years to follow, Bishop Allen and his wife, Sarah, operated a station on the Underground Railroad and assisted fugitive slaves. After Bishop Allen's elevation in the church, other major denominations began to loosen their grip on Black congregants, thereby setting the stage for the establishment of other Black churches, such as the African Methodist Episcopal Zion Church. The African-American church continued to grow through these "Black branches" or "sister churches," utilizing a similar form of governance to those of the parent churches.

As already noted, many freed Blacks preferred the Baptist and Methodist denominations. "The structure of the Baptist organization was more amenable to the existence of black churches and black preachers than was the system of government of any other denomination. Besides the Baptists, the Methodists were the only denominations to license black preachers with any frequency."[69] The Black churches in the North remained within the White-organized denominations. They had Black delegates attend the national convention and special meetings even though the Black delegates had no voting voice. As noted by one Methodist minister, the church polity at the time limited African-American participation, for "even in the midst of their brethren, they are made to feel that they are not one in Christ Jesus."[70]

GROWTH OF THE AFRICAN-AMERICAN CHURCH IN THE SOUTH

As in the North, to understand the post–Civil War growth of the African-American church in the South, we need to understand its pre–Civil War history.

The Baptist denomination predominantly shaped the African-American church of the South. Because of the slave revolts in the South, few if any Black independent churches existed, except for a sprinkling of AME and AME Zion churches. Before slavery, the messages from the slave owners' preachers were "sermons urging the slaves to be obedient and docile....

You slaves will go to heaven if you are good, but don't ever think that you will be close to your mistress and master. No! No! There will be a wall between you; but there will be holes in it that will permit you to look out and see your mistress when she passes by. If you want to sit behind this wall, you must do the language of the text 'Obey your masters.'"[71] Other messages talked about not lying and stealing, but told their listeners nothing about Jesus.

The White church struggled with doctrinal issues. The slaves were unable to rationalize biblically the brutality committed by the slave owners, and they lodged complaints of misconduct to the White church leadership. However, in the legal environment of the time, "to permit a slave to bring an accusation of misconduct against a white member was to contradict in the church the civil order where slave testimony against whites was legally unacceptable."[72] There was a great conflict of interest, because of how "church discipline could potentially complicate the slave-master relationship and how that relationship could in turn complicate church discipline."[73] In most cases, the church leadership acquitted the slave owner. Another concern in the slave community was slave marriage. Albert Raboteau posed these questions: "How could the church define breaches of the marital relation by slaves separated from their husbands and wives because of sale? Was it adultery for them to take up with another while their former spouses were still alive? The question becomes, 'What do we consider as a valid marriage between black people; and if any marriage be valid, is it in our fellowship to part them on any occasion?'"[74] In the eyes of these Blacks, the master's church and belief system had lost credibility.

After slavery, attendance in the White churches declined as freed Blacks established their own independent Black churches with Black preachers. Also, Methodist missionaries were active in establishing the Colored Methodist Churches (later to be renamed Christian Methodist Episcopal Churches). These churches were largely independent, with limited influence from White leaders.

THE PROTESTANT CHURCH MOVEMENT
AND THE AFRICAN-AMERICAN

In the aftermath of the Civil War, Protestants set about (1) rebuilding the denominational breaches brought on by the secession of the Southern states, and (2) using the nation's growing population of new immigrants as an opportunity to advance the Gospel message. Leading up to the Civil War, almost every major Protestant denomination had split over the slavery issue (the Episcopal Church distinguished itself by not succumbing to division), and with the conflict now behind them, these same denominations found it difficult to justify their respective theological stances and reunite. As a result, "the leaders of these various denominations decided to shore up the ecclesiastical organization, largely along lines inherited from Europe."[75] That is, they refused to deal with their differences head-on and instead settled for a form of peaceful coexistence. Other denominations remained separate from one another, though they remained unified on the theological issues of the Great Commandment and the Great Commission.

The independent Black churches began to form conventions and have national meetings. In 1895, three Black conventions—the Baptist Foreign Mission Convention, the National

Baptist Convention of America, and the National Baptist Education Convention—met in Atlanta, Georgia, to form the National Baptist Convention (NBC). This organization formed to unite Black Baptists nationwide. Later, turmoil existed in the ranks and eventually a split occurred with the formation of the National Baptist Convention of America in 1915. In 1961, the conservative stance over the issue of civil rights forced another split and the formation of the Progressive National Baptist Convention. The NBC remains the largest Black convention in the nation.

Can we have the conversation now? Another dialogue began between the Baptist churches in the North and the Baptist churches in the South—with a goal of working toward the unification of the churches. They could not agree over the slavery issue. A split occurred, and the Southern Baptist Convention (SBC) formed in 1845 with three hundred churches. After the Civil War, this predominantly White organization maintained a very conservative stance on race relations until the twenty-first century.

Lacking the resources to stay afloat, many smaller congregations (both Black and White) aligned themselves with the SBC. The ultra-conservative convention provided financial and other support to struggling churches, from which our Black churches benefited. However, the SBC prohibited Black churches from participating in the denomination's organizational structure or in any policy decision-making to effect change. Unable to bridge the racial divide or to bring about God's desire for unity and racial reconciliation, some Black churches resigned from the SBC while others remained active, anticipating future change of philosophy and spiritual breakthroughs.

The inability of the church to overcome these denominational rifts had a profound impact on the freed slaves. Regrettably, it allowed for the continuance of false theology, especially in the South. Many African-Americans found themselves separated from those who should have considered them brothers and sisters in Christ. The freedmen searched for a Gospel that applied Christian ethics to the social challenges they faced on a daily basis. The divided American church suffered further division.

As the country grew and the population expanded westward, missionaries began establishing African-American congregations in rural America. Most notable among these church plants were those of the Holiness and Pentecostal movements, and, more specifically, the Church of God in Christ, which has grown to become the largest African-American Pentecostal denomination in the United States. "Whereas, the churches begun prior to 1800 were essentially self-generated,...the churches that started after 1841 were much more the result of initiatives of denominations established within the prior period [1800-1841]."[76]

The focus of the predominately White Protestant church on the increasing population of immigrants coming to this country also had an impact on African-Americans. There were no government agencies on either the state or federal level to help the freed slaves assimilate into their society. Agencies of this sort were decades away, and the role of providing social assistance in mid-nineteenth-century America typically fell to the church. However, with the White churches concentrating their efforts on presenting the Gospel message to the nation's newcomers, both the newcomers and African-Americans found it difficult to navigate a myriad of social needs in a diverse and foreign cultural environment.

Spiritually, the inherited "strong community" concept engrained within the African culture would remain the driving force to support and sustain African-American culture in the years to come. For the stifled African-American experience, with its strong sense of community, a new component integrated a new "Seed of Hope": the Black church. Even in desolation, there would be consolation.

Now, it is worth noting a somewhat ironic twist: the striking difference between the plight of the freed slave and that of the recently arrived immigrant. Both lacked in certain basic skills (i.e., literacy and education), and each felt adrift in a new culture. However, the immigrants (largely of Western and Eastern European descent) found acceptance more quickly. To be clear, many of these new arrivals experienced abuse and discrimination, but their ability to adapt to the new environment was fast-tracked compared to that of the freed African-American slave. That is the irony. Though some slaves could claim a heritage within this country's borders from the time long before we had declared ourselves a nation, the European immigrant was able to adjust more quickly and easily to life in America. While many of us may have forgotten the struggles experienced by our African ancestors, many African-Americans today still feel a sense of alienation from the larger society, just as their ancestors did during the Reconstruction Era and beyond. Whether this is a reality or not, it is of little consequence. In matters of this nature, perception is often the reality with which we must deal.

With the influx of new arrivals on our shores, new religious observances took root. This served to compound our country's rapidly changing demographics. Coupled with the birth of so many fledgling church communities because of denominational differences and the inability of the church to meet the social needs of the family, one begins to understand that the possibility of a unified Protestant America was slowly disappearing. As a result, opportunities to reconcile across racial lines evaporated.

THE FIRST HALF OF THE
TWENTIETH CENTURY

In the twentieth century, living a life poisoned by violence, hatred, and indifference, Blacks sought relief and flocked to the big cities of the East and central Midwest, where major businesses were thriving. This influx into the new metropolises of the United States was not about escaping a past filled with slavery and segregation. There was something new on the horizon. For a man named Alain Locke, there was "a new vision of opportunity, of social and economic freedom, of a spirit to seize, even in the face of an extortionate and heavy toll, a chance for the improvement of conditions."[77] The movement brought together many people of African descent from all lifestyles: "the man from the city and the man from the town and village; the peasant, the student, the businessman, and the professional man; artist, poet, musician, adventurer, and worker; preacher and criminal, exploiter and social outcast…their greatest experience has been the finding of one another."[78]

It was peacetime. A community was born; it was a time of freedom of expression, a time of self-realization and actualization, of spiritual awakening and growth. It was "the Harlem Renaissance" (1918 to the mid-1930s). Harlem was a thriving center of Black culture for people of color. Locke lived it. He looked past the visible indicators of a diverse situation and saw the inner struggle of a people of destiny. For those on the outside looking in, he says, "The American Negroes have been a race more in name than in fact, or to be exact, more in sentiment than in experience."[79] For those within our culture, Locke saw that "the chief bond between them has been that of a common condition rather than a common consciousness; a problem in common rather than a life in common."[80] The Harlem Renaissance bore witness to an explosion in arts, literature, education, activism, inventions, and collaborations previously unknown to the country.

Even radio and the newspaper became door openers that allowed African-Americans to surface in the limelight. Radios tuned to the championship boxing matches of Jack Johnson and Joe Louis and the baseball games of Jackie Robinson. Olympic winners Jesse Owens and Alice Coachman; singers such as Paul Robeson, Lena Horne, and Ella Fitzgerald; gospel singers such as Mahalia Jackson and the Five Blind Boys of Mississippi; great musicians such as Count Basie and Duke Ellington; and literary geniuses like Langston Hughes and Zora Neale Hurston took center stage. In meeting halls were birthed great orators and preachers such as Adam Clayton Powell, Sr., and Thurgood Marshall. The great educator Cain Hope Felder, the spiritual mystic Howard Thurman (mentor to Dr. Martin Luther King, Jr.), and intellectual pursuits, such as the debate team of Wiley College, all drew attention to Black successes. That is just naming a few. There were also social activists such as A. Philip Randolph, Marcus Garvey, and W. E. B. DuBois; scientists such as George Washington Carver and entrepreneur Madam C. J. Walker; and educational visionaries such as Mary McLeod Bethune, Booker T. Washington, and other former slaves who joined together to found educational institutions of higher learning such as Morris Brown College in Atlanta. Then there was the creation, in 1926, of Negro History Week by Carter G. Woodson—now known as Black History Month. These are just some of our gifts to this nation.

Every new accomplishment became a means to quiet the inner rage at the depravity and neglect aimed at—and felt by—the African-American community. Each blow to the opponent, every win across the finish line, every home run, every achievement award, every hit song, and every stand for righteousness was a strike against racial inequality and the status quo as African-Americans began to break through the color barriers and rise as stars and role models for future generations.

We were telling our story. Maybe there was a time in your life when you lived in the liminal space of betwixt and between—where the fog of ambiguity was your friend, and it just did not make sense. What was the story of your family of origin? Maybe you need to share it with others. As for the Harlem Renaissance, group expression and self-determination were a lived-out consequence of life and African-American expression continued to be a benefit and blessing to America.

A new song, "Lift Every Voice and Sing," crystallized this new sense of divine triumph. Written by James Weldon Johnson in 1900, this song carries the title "the Black National Anthem." The lyrics chronicle our journey and keep hope alive.

Lift Every Voice and Sing

(Verse 1)

Lift every voice and sing, 'til earth and heaven ring,
Ring with the harmonies of liberty;
Let our rejoicing rise, high as the listening skies,
Let it resound loud as the rolling sea.

(Chorus 1)

Sing a song full of the faith that the dark past has taught us,
Sing a song full of the hope that the present has brought us;
Facing the rising sun of our new day begun,
Let us march on 'til victory is won.

(Verse 2)

Stony the road we trod, bitter the chastening rod,
Felt in the days when hope unborn had died;
Yet with a steady beat, have not our weary feet
Come to the place for which our fathers sighed?

(Chorus 2)

We have come over a way that with tears has been watered,
We have come, treading our path through the blood of the slaughtered,
Out from the gloomy past, 'til now we stand at last
Where the white gleam of our bright star is cast.

(Verse 3)

God of our weary years, God of our silent tears,
Thou who has brought us thus far on the way;
Thou who has by Thy might, Led us into the light,
Keep us forever in the path, we pray.

(Chorus 3)

Lest our feet stray from the places, our God, where we met Thee,
Lest, our hearts drunk with the wine of the world, we forget Thee;
Shadowed beneath Thy hand, may we forever stand,
True to our God, true to our native land.[81]

World War I began in 1914. The entire country was devastated, and along with others, African-Americans answered
the call to serve once again. They patriotically enlisted. "Maybe
they will accept us now" was the underlying sentiment. *This
is my country, too.* The African-American soldiers served well,
segregated into substandard barracks to fight a war and return
to a home where little had changed. Hope deferred. In some
states of this nation, the honorably discharged Black soldier
who gave his life for his country could not vote.

The Wall Street crash, the Great Depression of the 1930s,
Women's Suffrage, Prohibition, and the growth of labor unions
followed swiftly after the war. In the meantime, inventions and
scientific advances in media and communications progressed.
(Appendix A contains a list of African-American inventors and
inventions.) Nonetheless, with the influx of immigrants to this
country, there was a sense of abject poverty that threatened the
family unit. Jobs were scarce not only for African-Americans,
but for all Americans.

In the 1930s, under President Roosevelt's New Deal, the
Works Progress Administration funded by Congress provided
jobs for vast numbers of the unemployed. One of the New
Deal's projects employed writers and researchers to interview
and document the stories of freed African-American slaves.
Even for ex-slaves who had no ability to read and write, our

heavenly Father provided a means to document our history and journey for posterity. Chronicled for all times were the shared experiences of abuse and dehumanization for these people of color.

POST-DEPRESSION DEVELOPMENTS

Searching for remedies to our plight, African-American organizations such as the National Association for the Advancement of Colored People (NAACP),[82] the National Urban League, the National Council of Negro Woman, the Universal Negro Improvement Association, the Black Methodist for Church Renewal, and the Nation of Islam rallied to our cry.

In December 1941, a national atrocity occurred when the Japanese bombed Pearl Harbor, causing the United States to enter into World War II. The national issues of justice and equality again had to take a back seat. The country mobilized the troops, and once again, African-Americans, both male and female, enlisted. Unlike World War I, where Black soldiers often worked as cargo handlers and cooks, World War II provided new, more prominent roles for Black soldiers on the field of battle. The U.S. Army Air Corps trained the first group of Black pilots, known as the Tuskegee Airmen, who flew supply missions, service missions, and bombing missions in North Africa and Europe. "In 1944 they began flying with the white pilots…successfully running bombing missions and becoming the only U.S. unit to sink a German destroyer."[83]

World War II ended in 1945, and the fight for freedom and social justice persisted. Our troops returned home to a ticker-tape parade…and then, again, to joblessness. President

Harry S. Truman signed Executive Order 9981 to desegregate the U.S. Armed Forces in 1948—only after the end of the war. This was a step in the right direction but at great cost to human life. No one wins in wartime.

THE CIVIL RIGHTS MOVEMENT

Throughout this treatise, we see how corrective measures to make African-Americans an integral part of American society and the church met with opposition from the ruling class. The African-American held title to full citizenry in the United States—but in name only, as Congress enacted corrective measures almost impossible to implement.

It was peacetime in December 1955 in Montgomery, Alabama, when Rosa Parks refused to give up her seat for a White passenger on a bus. On that day, she said, "No." This event fueled the Civil Rights Movement, the chief herald of which was Dr. Martin Luther King, Jr. He was, and still is, a hero of the faith to both African-Americans and many White Americans alike.

Not long after that, President Dwight D. Eisenhower signed into law the Civil Rights Act of 1957, the first civil rights legislation since the Reconstruction Era. The newly formed Commission on Civil Rights and the Civil Rights Division of the Justice Department would investigate allegations of minority citizens' deprivation of their rights, especially the right to vote. See the list of political decisions that have affected African-Americans since 1948 on page 81.

A shift was on the horizon. It was a shift in the mind and not the heart. Governmental control changed as the Democrat John F. Kennedy, a senator from Massachusetts, was

---

Major Political Decisions That Affected African-Americans

Year	Political Decisions
1948	President Harry Truman signed an executive order to desegregate the U.S. Armed Forces.
1954	The U.S. Supreme Court decision, *Brown v. the Board of Education*, stated that separate education facilities are inherently unequal.
1964	The Civil Rights Act prohibited discrimination in education and employment based on race, color, religion, or national origin.
1965	President Lyndon B. Johnson issued Executive Order 11246, directing that all government contracting agencies "take affirmative action to ensure that applicants are employed...without regard to their race, color, religion, sex, or national origin."
1970	The U.S. Department of Labor issued Order Number 4, authorizing goals and timetables to correct the "underutilization" of minorities by federal contractors.
1978	In the Bakke decision, the U.S. Supreme Court upheld the use of race as a legitimate factor in admitting students to colleges and universities, but ruled against the use of quotas or targeted minimums.
1996	Voters passed California 209, abolishing all public-sector affirmative action programs in the state.

elected president in 1960. The rise of racial tensions persisted and forced President Kennedy to make good on his campaign promises to African-Americans prior to his election. The greatest impact of his response came from the push to hire and promote African-Americans in the governmental sector. This contrasted with then-existing practices of many major corporations and labor unions, who were maintaining the traditional ways of doing business. Not only that, the heightened awareness of discrimination and public opinion polls awakened the nation. Dr. Martin Luther King, Jr.'s nonviolent strategy of peaceful protests, boycotts, and sit-ins was paying off.

Sadly, President Kennedy was assassinated on November 22, 1963, before he could summon further congressional support. Nevertheless, the Civil Rights Act of 1964 passed in both the House and the Senate under President Lyndon B. Johnson. "Its implementation eventually defined the meaning of equal employment opportunity and affirmative action."[84] With President Kennedy's death, President Johnson's eyes were on the next election. He had to demonstrate to the nation that he had broken away from traditional Southern views on the race issue, and in September 1965, he signed into law Executive Order 11246, which ordered the end of discrimination in the federal government—another kernel of popcorn falls to the ground.

HEAR MY MOTHER'S JOURNEY IN THE WORKPLACE AND AT HOME

As for me, I exhaled. This decision was a triumph in our household; seeing colorism addressed was a victory for us. My mother was dark in complexion, and for many years, she trained Whites and light-complexioned Black employees for promotions at the government's Department of Health, Education, and Welfare, while she remained overlooked. After the executive order, her name was one of the first to make the list for a promotion. Nonetheless, the toll of her journey had its effects. While still being able to work and carry the responsibility of providing for our entire family, including her mother and other relatives, she had become a closet alcoholic. I was so happy to finally see my mother get the promotion and recognition that she deserved. "Upward mobility" was its name. Finally, the doors of opportunity were open, and many people of color, including women, were benefiting. However, the doors were not opening for everyone.

With Dr. King's relentless pursuit for justice and equality for all, the church rallied for the first time in many years. On April 4, 1968, Dr. King was assassinated at the Lorraine Motel in Memphis, Tennessee. On that day, the country witnessed the inner rage of generations of denial, rejection, and neglect that came full circle. The world bore witness to our struggle. Rioting and looting erupted. In the wake of recovery, Dr. King's dream of freedom still lives on in the hearts of every African-American today. In the face of adversity, noted leaders such as Percy Sutton, Jesse Jackson, Al Sharpton, and Dorothy Height kept on bombarding the office of the presidency, congressional representatives, and big businesses with demands to formulate strategies to combat racial inequality and corrective measures to fight social injustices under the law.

It would be years later before another incident captured the nation by surprise. The year was 1991. In California, a Black man named Rodney King sustained a brutal assault by two police officers, and someone videotaped the incident. How long can one oppress the marginalized people's passion for freedom? What will be the next racial atrocity; how long before someone will sound the alarm? The reaction to King's beating was widespread and passionate, resulting in rioting across the city of Los Angeles. Some saw the riots as malicious, senseless acts of destruction when "rioting and violence is the language

of the unheard,"[85] speaking out after the long years of victimization. Is there no balm in Gilead? For those police officers in
1991, what kind of rage reigned in their hearts to render such a
dispensation of evil? This volume does not excuse the behavior
or actions of any people group, but it highlights residue that
lives beneath the surface of our flesh. Many (and this could be
anyone) have lived a life bereft of a sense of belonging. Feelings
of cultural detachment, societal influences, and media mockery
exist in a hidden heart unknown to humankind. When pushed
to the limits, there is a response. Jesus invites us to "Come."
When humankind is incapable of doing God's will, sin prevails,
and believers must look to the Word of God as a light and a
lamp. When will we cry out to the Lord:

> Search me [thoroughly], O God, and know my heart;
> test me, and know my anxious thoughts; and see if there
> is any wicked or hurtful way in me, and lead me in the
> everlasting way.
> —PSALM 139:23-24, AMP

The conversation did happen, and in 1995, the Southern
Baptist Convention acknowledged their years of impropriety.
They enacted a public resolution "denouncing racism and re-
pudiating its past defense of slavery and opposition to the civil
rights movement."[86] By 2012, the SBC elected its first Black
president, Fred Luter, Jr., whose goal in his term in office was
to build racial harmony and diversity within the organization.
Again, *Can we have the conversation?* This was a major milestone
in Christendom in the United States. There is more to come.

A rally cry was brewing in the deep. Years later, another superhero emerged, and again the African-American heart
quieted. Affirming hope, people of color were encouraged by

the vote in November 2008. In January 2009, President Barack Obama's inauguration as the forty-fourth president of the United States of America, a person of color, changed history. Rejected, derided, disrespected, and belittled by the Republican Party and others, the courageous president kept his hand to the wheel for two terms and brought improved medical care, and fought terrorism by ordering the capture of Osama bin Laden. This resulted in bin Laden's death and the eventual weakening of the terrorist group Al-Qaeda. Faced with the legacy of his predecessor—a plummeting automobile industry and the recession of 2007—Obama fought hard to restore this nation and its faith in the American dream. This did not come without a cost. The country rebelled, and the Democratic Party suffered major losses during reelections in the House of Representatives and the Senate. After President Obama's second term in office ended, the Republican Party held the majority seats in the House of Representatives and the Senate. The nation was at a crossroads, for this vicious roadblock rendered the bipartisan approach inept, and the people suffered for it. In time, the economy recovered. What had the American people learned? Will we again repeat history? Has our moral barometer become desensitized? When can we, together, come to the table and have the dialogue?

The 2016 election came and went. Some who were weary of the standoff in Congress, volatile media coverage, etc., cherished a belief in their hearts for a better America. President Donald Trump took office, and another mindset took the scene and stirred the suppressed, buried feelings of the majority culture, reawakening strong concerns about the state of the nation. Fear and anxiety began to plague another segment of the population; just as there was a rise in racism during President Obama's presidency, "a rise in hate-crimes has been tied to President Trump's victory."[87] Many took to the streets in protest, while others conversed in cyberspace or were paralyzed waiting for the outcome. President Trump's supporters saw in their candidate "their best chance to dampen the most painful blows of globalization and trade, to fight special interests, and to be heard and protected."[88] We will not forget his stance on immigration and his passion to "Make America Great Again."

Now let us look again. Although African-Americans were not the main target of President Trump's campaign, an article from the *Intelligence Report* identified the "rise in the membership of other hate groups such as the anti-Muslim... neo-Confederate groups...Klan groups, neo-Nazi...white Nationalists...the racist skinheads...LGBT and black Separatist groups."[89] Then, there was the rise of those who were antagonistic toward multiculturalism. Core national issues such as gun control, globalization, labor, and anti-government patriots became of heightened concern post-election. Overall, these extremist groups understood that while President Trump might not fully endorse their position, he was still a catalyst to their cause.

It was clear we were at a crossroads, and the question that rang out was "Oh, church, what say ye?"

The history of the African-American people is only one story and one journey. There are many other stories. Won't you share? Let us build the bridge together, for without you there is no reconciliation.

FOUR LET'S TAKE A CLOSER LOOK

Rebuilding our lives can be painful, yet it can be done. There are many losses—fires, floods, storms, natural disasters, pandemics; then there is war, invasion, assault, and crime. As image bearers of God, we have the resilience to fight back, to rebuild, to restore, to reconstruct, and to reconnect.

1. Our life experiences are ever changing. Sometimes, we find out that we have to start afresh. What was that experience like for you?

2. We all struggle. Where have you found the most freedom?

3. Sometimes when life is tough, we drift into isolation and alienation. Try to put words into what you have understood so far.

FIVE

Psychological Wounds of Slavery: Sacred Secrets and Identity

> I appeal to you therefore, brothers and sisters, by the mercies of God, to present your bodies as a living sacrifice, holy and acceptable to God, which is your spiritual worship. Do not be conformed to this world, but be transformed by the renewing of your minds, so that you may discern what is the will of God—what is good and acceptable and perfect.
> —ROMANS 12:1-2, NRSV

NOW WE HAVE a better view of the African-American journey in the United States and the effects of their post–Civil War experience. Let us turn to the four wounds mentioned in the first chapter that have affected the African-American's ability to build strong roots in America. They are:

- Identity
- Sacred Secrets
- Powerlessness/Rage
- Mistrust

It is important to understand these factors in light of our changing society and religious influences before we turn toward the healing possibilities of Spiritual Formation, reclaiming our traditions, and then having the conversation. There is no possibility of healing for anyone without first having a thorough understanding of the nature of the injury.

We will discuss the first two factors in this chapter, and the second two in the next chapter.

In December 2009, I visited the California Science Center in Los Angeles to view the American Anthropological Association's exhibit "RACE: Are We So Different?" They designed the exhibit to promote discovery, discussion, and reflection on how the American individualistic worldview over the past three hundred years has shaped our minds and our thinking today about race. On that day, I saw adults and parents with children move from one exhibit to another, learning and teaching each other. Yet, there was one story in particular that got my attention.

> In that story, a Southern White American male, about forty, talked about an experience in his childhood that occurred around the 1940s when he was about nine years old. He told of a senior citizen, named Miss Helen, who took it upon herself to teach the children in the neighborhood social graces, which included how to speak properly to adults. The children learned not to call adults by their first names, but to use either "Mr." or "Mrs." before it. One day as he looked outside, he saw a gardener in Miss Helen's yard, an older Negro man about age seventy. Showing what he had learned

from Miss Helen, he asked his name. The gentleman responded "Joe," and the child proceeded to call him Mr. Joe. Miss Helen, watching from afar, inquired in her sweet voice, "Son, what are you doing?" and the child responded proudly, "I was talking with Mr. Joe." He was proud to show Miss Helen that he was listening and had responded as she had taught him. Miss Helen then corrected the innocent child. "Oh no, son, he's the gardener. He is just n----- Joe." The child turned to Mr. Joe to see his response and Mr. Joe did not respond. From that day on, the child referred to him as n----- Joe, or as "Miss Helen's gardener" or "the gardener" (both more depersonalizing forms of address).

First, when the young boy asked the gardener his name, he responded "Joe." In those days, this was a safe response. Our journey begins here. One statement can change a life. When the nine-year-old changes the way he addresses the gardener, we find that Mr. Joe's silence and invisibility aroused within that child an unearned sense of validity, privilege, and entitlement, which he carried on into his adult life. It reinforced the child's mistaken belief, given to him by his culture, in the form of people like Miss Helen, that he had a superiority that was innate to him due to his race—inborn and not earned. Then, another trigger, an encounter with a coworker, brought this incident to his remembrance, and he began to reflect on it. He regretted it and became more aware of himself holistically. According to Derald Wing Sue, "Research supports the belief that racial awakening is most likely to occur when people encounter situations, events, and/or experiences that challenge their preconceived notions, beliefs, or values."[90] This awakening could occur to anyone at any time. The question for each of us is: Will we meet this awakening with a willing heart? We must also ask ourselves, What are our next steps toward recovery and responsibility?

Mr. Joe, Miss Helen's gardener, did not have the opportunity to take advantage of modern resources like therapy or small groups. Yet, we commend him for surviving the backlash of insignificance while holding his ground. His silence eventually influenced the young White boy in his manhood, helping him to unearth inner personal truths about his own privilege. I cannot help but wonder how Mr. Joe himself processed that event. In his silence, I wonder what secrets lay beneath a heart torn.

> More recently, I heard the story of a talented young woman. This young woman has a PhD, is an accomplished author, and is highly sought after for workshops and other speaking engagements. She went to the hospital to sit at the bedside of her father. She heard these words from his lips for the first time: "It was worth it." She did not know what to make of it, so she smiled. Later, she found out that her father was a survivor. He came from a poor family, one of twelve. As a youth, he worked the cotton fields and sawmills. His work ethic continued into his adult life and now exists in his daughter. Like any daughter, she desired her father's attention and his love as she was growing up. When she did not receive it, she felt neglected. Other people seemed to get more of his time than she did. Therefore, she

focused her energy on her education. Nonetheless, she later learned that, deep inside, he had a parental fear of her misuse, and in his own way, he tried to protect her.[91]

Even in this seemingly toxic father-daughter relationship, I would like to believe that there was a look, a smile, a hug, or some other intangible moments of deep affection and conviction that may have gone unnoticed. When I look back at my own life, I know I misinterpreted some of the subtle nuances; I missed some of those times of connectedness even within my own family.

SACRED SECRETS

The prior scenarios provide examples of inner truths from the heart that were unknown, undetected, or suppressed in the person who carried them. Oh! How I wish our society would just slow down. Let us formulate the definition of the first cultural conditioning factor under discussion—*sacred secrets* is defined as "personal, valued information unknown to others or hidden from others" (and "others" sometimes includes us). This privileged information could originate within the family or from our preferences, lifestyles, or experiences or from society in general—*dare we to share*. Hidden and suppressed, these thoughts and images can surface at any time, depending on the triggers. For the African-American psyche, once exposed, they can drive an emotional response in some visible and tangible way. We all have them.

The episode of the Southern man, who interacted with Miss Helen and Mr. Joe as a boy, aroused feelings related to events playing out in his adult life. Though he could no longer deny the presence of bias in himself, the question remains, How did he respond to this occurrence?

Though we never hear Mr. Joe respond to the young boy, in inner silence, every African-American can sense his heartbeat. Even for the freedman, the psychological dimension of slavery was present. We can learn much from Mr. Joe's silence that day. Think about it. Some may refer to it as the "silence of the lamb." Underneath lies, to paraphrase the words of Derald Wing Sue, an "innocent demeanor laboring under a false sense to be obedient, threats and duress or deprivation characterized by a loss of dignity and respect."[92] Both create undesirable and hurtful conditions that could upset the prospects of survival for any people group. It is worth wondering if Mr. Joe and the boy who interacted with him (now an adult) wore or wear many of the same hats—parent, grandparent, uncle, brother, nephew. Incidents like these affect the care and nurture of the entire family. I wonder, what were the spiritual and psychological effects of enduring these racial slurs and slights? We may never know. However, at the end of the day, we can be sure that implicit and explicit bias affect the care and nurture of those we love most—especially our families.

Blacks used silence—a subtle peaceful coexistence or a guarded protective appearance—to achieve their aim. Underneath the silence is the accumulated inner pain and wounds of hundreds of years that result in a soul shutting down secretively. During and after slavery, African-Americans survived by living in a false self-identity, a camouflage, "to veil a manipulative, hostile personality in a look of laziness, subservience, and loyalty."[93] Herskovits, writing around the

1950s, acknowledges that "the Negroes…in concealing their faults from their owners, make no inquiry, elicit no information; no one feels at liberty to disclose the transgressor; appear profoundly ignorant; the matter assumes the sacredness of a 'professional secret'; for they remember that they may hereafter require the same concealment of their own transgressions from their fellow servants."[94] In the midst of discrimination, segregation, and physical and personal attacks, these tactics were painful yet invaluable. The quietness was not always hopeless, but helpful when God's Word of confidence and comfort could secure them: "I WILL NEVER DESERT YOU, NOR WILL I EVER FORSAKE YOU" (Hebrews 13:5b, NASB). Trusting in these words, African-Americans remained grounded in the struggle.

Nevertheless, a modern-day alternative view exists among Black Americans. Consider these words from Dorothy S. Ruiz: "The issues and concerns of blacks today are basically the same as they were three decades ago; the most imminent ones center around achievement and advancement…but the primary… factors that have hampered the achievement and advancement of blacks are racism and discrimination."[95] In reality, I agree that these long-standing issues stifle the African-American's developmental years in this country. We are the most advanced nation in this world, yet we must ask the question: Where is the love? As we continue in this dialogue, we must recognize that the most catastrophic of all challenges for African-Americans is "the often changing demands of the dominant culture… that affect the way in which African-Americans respond to the need for dignity, love, nurturing, and respect by the individual members."[96] I would also include additional matters of the heart—namely, the lack of affirmation and acceptance. Other at-risk areas within the African-American community concern parenting and managing interpersonal relationships.

THE RELATIONAL ASPECTS
OF SACRED SECRETS

Sacred secrets divide into two categories: (1) externally, these are secrets kept from "outsiders" but known by most family members, and (2) internally, the secrets kept from other family members. (We will ignore, for now, the secrets an individual might keep from himself or herself.)

The fear of exposing these sacred secrets or myths is particularly toxic when unresolved family issues exist. Personal family relationships are labeled as "nobody's business but our own" or "don't ask; don't tell" because of a legacy of mistrust. African-Americans often teach their children at a very young age to keep family business within the family or not to "air dirty laundry in public." These secrets range from informal adoption, fatherhood, and unwed pregnancy to mental health issues, abuse, alcoholism, drugs, homosexuality, generational traits, and skin color issues. Some of the visible contributors to sacred secrets are mental illness, HIV/AIDS, abortions, or the lack of medical treatment (the last is especially high among African-American males). Let us swing the pendulum to the other side. I have already spoken of national issues that have escalated in the form of riots and protest—these are a more vivid pronouncement and exposure of emotions and feelings unexplored.

One of the most striking examples of sacred secrets I have encountered was in the unspoken message that I came across when a concerned son sought answers about his father.

He related that his father died and, in his belongings, they found a distinguished medal—the Purple Heart. His father had never mentioned this to anyone, not even his mother. The son could not understand why his father hid this great and noble accomplishment from the family.[97]

This information about his father would have been beneficial to a son finding his way in life, feeling bereft of a relationship shaped by love. For the son, this discovery was a missed opportunity to connect with his father. For the father, what unspoken secrets lay within?

The why of the "sacred secrets" is the question that hovers and one that only the Spirit of the living God can answer.

IDENTITY—WHO AM I?

For this section, I define *identity* as "the way one describes oneself and that which shapes one's core beliefs and values, which drives how one thinks and what one believes." As the majority culture continued to exclude African-Americans from virtually every aspect of our society, a distinct cultural identity began to take shape. As Nancy Boyd-Franklin observes, "One of the most devastating outcomes of the legacy of slavery and oppression is the feeling of rejection that many black people experience today."[98] When we think about identity, the factors we consider can be listed as "who they are," "the way they think about themselves," "the way they are viewed by the world," and "the characteristics that define them." However, we are dealing here with more than mere thoughts and feelings. It was the *reality* of the freed slave's exclusion and rejection that eventually changed the behavior of an entire people. It did not change their spiritual identity in relationship to God.

As Boyd-Franklin notes, "'resistance and suspicion' or 'healthy cultural paranoia' were the glue that many black families developed over generations in response to oppression. Often it takes the form of a refusal to identify with and trust persons differing from themselves in color, life-style, class values, and so on."[99] Thus, we can more clearly understand how the African-American "identity" began to take shape, and it was this constant state of living in a false self-identity, a camouflage, to veil a manipulative and hostile dual identity that contributed greatly to the inability of African-Americans to feel "rooted" in American society. As we can see from looking back on history, this rejection-based identity had a profound social and political impact. Further, it prevented African-American believers from feeling fully accepted, affirmed, and secure in their identity in Christ.

SKIN COLOR ISSUES

One such psychological aspect within the African-American culture is something very physical: skin color. During the years of slavery, many "mulatto" or light-skinned children, raised in the homes of the plantation owners, were the products of rape. They became house servants with special liberties within the plantation system, unlike the darker-complexioned slaves who worked in the field. This was another way to divide and conquer—just another form of prejudice. It created friction between slaves in the "big house" and slaves in the field or between light-skinned and dark-skinned African-Americans. Even the White standard of beauty imposed throughout slavery time was contrary to the African's sense of beauty in the dark: Black skin color. As a result, colorism, a class system that favored light-skinned individuals over the darker complexioned, brought internal rivalry, envy, and bitterness in the Black community. This onslaught happens when a dark-complexioned man chooses to marry a lighter-complexioned female, so his kids will not experience the same shame and disgrace he did, or "children growing up feeling that they lack something critically important for happiness and success if they are not white or at least of a light skin color."[100] Even today, subtle comments among African-American women about "good hair" and "bad hair" still occur, and many hide behind wigs, hairpieces, extensions, and eyelashes, chasing the American dream. The above examples show the depth of the oppressive acts of slavery, still playing out in real life.

In the post–Civil War South, to cope with skin color issues, unemployment, exploitation, and stringent controls, many citizens immigrated to the West or the North in search of acceptance and a better life. Others went to the urban areas, where they could become invisible among the already large number of African-American residents, while some were able to pass as White and did just that. With the raising of the African-American consciousness during the Civil Rights movement and the advent of an anti-Christian culture that denies absolute truth and rejects scientific and philosophical truths, this skin color classism has diminished.

Now, if only modern parents would address these cultural conditioning factors early in the child's development. When their children come face-to-face with stereotypes, and external and internal biases, they would be better equipped and prepared to embrace their uniqueness and prevail over oppression and deprivation. They should be free to live to their full potential.

As Christians, we are overcomers. We must see these stereotypes and biases as an opportunity to combat evil with good. This is a sort of proactive love of neighbor as we make a choice to carry our cross and follow Christ rather than follow the ways of the world. We must love others as God loves us. We cannot simply receive God's love and stop there. If Jesus is the Lord of our lives, then our lives should reflect His example. We live in the *Imago Dei* as He lived.

"Too often, black children do not grow up with the understanding that it is all right to be different and that skin color is only one of the many ways in which people differ."[101] More importantly, "the black child has been forced to live in two cultures—her own minority culture and the majority one. He has had to teach himself to contain his aggression around whites while freely expressing it among blacks."[102] Regardless, "unlike other cultures or ethnic groups who can 'blend in' or become part of the 'melting pot,' black people by virtue of their skin color are visible reminders of the inequities of society."[103]

The spiritual implications of coldheartedness here are catastrophic. Only time will tell whether our children will adopt our religious convictions and actually live them out in life. Will they merely accept Jesus as Savior or see Him also as Lord? Will they become "imitators of Christ" or imitators of the status quo? We must continue to pray.

RACISM AND EDUCATION

The majority ruling class would prefer to believe the following:

- That racism does not exist in America
- That the African-American struggle is over
- That the issue of identity and racial equality is an issue of class
- That African-Americans are claiming the victim role and crying wolf
- That claims of reverse discrimination are real and justified (as an example, see the Bakke decision on the table on page 81)

No one wants to think of himself or herself as racist, and because of that, avoidance and denial become a means of validating the false self by not facing the truth. In spite of it all, Black Americans have made progress. Some are homeowners. We have access to medical care; we are educated, maintain jobs, are entrepreneurs; we are politicians, serve in the government; we are involved in social media, the entertainment industry, as well as the church—and there is more to do. Nevertheless, we still suffer from the glass ceiling; inequities exist in law enforcement, court decisions, and the prison system. Blacks and Latinos serve more time than their White counterparts for the same crime, and still African-Americans continue to have trouble in relating to their fellow citizens. This is the area where the Black family and the disciplines and traditions of the Black church have buffered the painful emotions of African-Americans. They have been foundational to the African-American's development.

Initially, to prove ourselves, African-Americans believed the answer was education. African-Americans made headway as major denominations, societies, and associations across the nation contributed toward building educational systems for the freedmen. In addition to financial support, the church provided in-kind support of teachers and field missionary workers. Because of that investment, historical Black colleges and universities (HBCUs) are still in existence today. There is Wilberforce University, Morgan State University (Methodists), Morehouse College (Baptists), Fisk University, Howard University (Congregationalists), Knoxville College (Presbyterians), and Prairie View A&M University, to name a few. Because of such educational institutions, literacy among African-Americans increased monumentally. In time, African-American Christians established their own institutions and seminaries, such as Lane College, Livingstone College, and the struggling Morris Brown College. These institutions maintained a structure similar to their White counterparts and developed their own fraternities, sororities, clubs, and associations.[104] For some college students who are of the African diaspora, the poem "Invictus," by William Ernest Henley, written in 1875, became their battle cry: "I am the master of my fate; I am the captain of my soul."[105]

Once they were educated, they believed acceptance would follow. In spite of their educational achievements, the racist practices of the established educational institutions, including Christian schools and seminaries, remained unchanged. Segregated policies and stringent enrollment practices denied admission to the poor and underprivileged people of color. This circumstance forced African-American youth to seek educational institutions where they could learn and excel. As a response, Black studies programs and other outlets for African-Americans within the fields of the arts and literature emerged, providing a means of self-expression, self-awareness, and self-fulfillment. These advances illuminated the rich heritage of our culture once denied us and set the stage for self-identification and freedom of expression.

Overall, education gave African-Americans a new, far-reaching voice in society and a platform for equality. As time passed, the White Christian educational institutions and seminaries implemented major policy changes affecting enrollment—a decision long in coming. Only time will tell if the White Christian seminaries and educational systems have spiritually awakened to become a healthy diverse cultural learning environment, or just a status quo mock-up. The jury is still out.

FIVE LET'S TAKE A CLOSER LOOK

This chapter was filled with many stories. We have identified some cultural conditioning factors that affect us all. Wounds hurt. It does not matter whether they are known or unknown, understood or misunderstood. Often, we disconnect or hide or avoid. Sometimes we are in denial. And often we do not know why.

1. Let's reflect. What, if anything, presented in this chapter are you having a hard time understanding?

2. How do you relate to the slights or uncomfortable statements others make in your presence?

3. As you think about the conditioning factors—sacred secrets and identity—what comes to mind in your own life? Jot it down.

SIX

Psychological Wounds of Slavery: Powerlessness/Rage and Mistrust

I know why the caged bird sings. He sings for you.

—Anonymous

IN THIS CHAPTER, we will look at the second pair of our four cultural conditioning factors: powerlessness/rage and mistrust.

POWERLESSNESS/RAGE

For our purposes, we will define the cultural conditioning factor of *powerlessness/rage* as "the state of lacking power, combined with sudden and extreme outbursts of anger." As we look at this cultural conditioning factor, we will examine a concept known as microaggressions, which are hurtful attitudes and behaviors endured by minorities. For examples of these microaggressions, we will examine some statements and short conversations between Whites and Blacks and other ethnic groups in this area. We will find that the thoughts and belief systems of both groups are impacted. A closer look at a deeper level will expose how other cultural conditioning factors play a role in subduing the behavior and hearts of the privileged and the marginalized.

For African-Americans, slavery and its aftermath are always the foundational factors that set the mind and the mindset into motion. Powerlessness and rage do not occur in a vacuum all by themselves. We do not always know what triggers the actual explosion in an outburst of rage. Nor are we always conscious of the stimulus of the previous cultural conditioning factors—*sacred secrets* (nuggets of information hidden by the family and others) or *identity* (a set of characteristics that are unique to oneself)—that undergird our mindset and act as a catalyst to incite our emotions. We do know that some of the triggers to rage are spiritual in nature and born out of years of oppression and domination by the ruling class.

The efforts of the ruling class have not proved successful in addressing many of the social problems in this country. People of color still struggle with economic and social issues such as "unemployment and underemployment (last hired, first fired), economic instability, the invisibility of black men, poverty, separation, out-of-wedlock births, delinquency, crime, domestic violence, child abuse, alcoholism, poor health, AIDS, educational failure and high dropout rates."[106] In addition, let us not forget the human trafficking of youth and teens—a system that kidnaps and places into forced prostitution both female and male.

When it comes to the failures of the ruling class to address psychological and social problems in this country, our school system is a case in point. As an example, the No Child Left Behind Act of 2002 (NCLB) under the George W. Bush Administration was the government's way to address achievement gaps in education for the English-language learner, students in special education, and the poor and minority students (primarily Black and Latino). Yes, there were successes with increased test scores nationally, but the program did not yield the desired results of producing equal opportunities for all students. Some state schools lacked equitable funding for desired program success, especially in the poor communities. Educational systems placed underperforming students in special programs by the fourth-grade level. The subliminal message from the social conditions listed above had already had an adverse effect in the young child's conscious mind and sometimes would impede the learning process. The message to students was subtle but damaging—"you are dumb; you have no value"—while peer pressure and bullying prevailed. Some students became hyperactive and entered classes with the slower learners. Boyd-Franklin believes that in these learning environments "a disproportionate number of black children, particularly boys, [were] placed...on Ritalin"[107] to calm active students in a teaching environment of fear and mistrust. There are more problems within the education system; we have only highlighted one area.

Overall, wherever there are inequities, the people suffer. In 2015, the Every Student Succeeds Act (ESSA) replaced NCLB. It closed some of the gaps and included more accountability. They needed a more community-based approach. Early intervention programs developed, which included parental involvement. It allowed the states more flexibility in the learning process by providing funding and state programs for low-performing schools, gathering input from parents and families, and expanding the law to address students with disabilities. Though the main work of raising children begins at home, these family-connected educational interventions are more positive than methods previously employed.

Second, these economic indicators listed above also affect the family. The wound starts early. Our children, as young as preschool, feel the effects of these factors, because these factors create an environment of fear and rejection. They can sense that something is different, but the cause of the sensation is unknown to them. In addition, powerlessness and rage have contributed to the breakup of numerous Black families and to the fragile nature of some family units. Even providing nurturing or empathy for African-Americans can be complex without an understanding of the history and the culture of this derailed social group. Then, there are childhood emotions, childhood experiences, differing parenting styles, cultural issues, changing demographics, and an inherent mindset that too often goes unexamined.

> Let us look at one such example of a family in crisis. Our case study here, drawn from the writings of William H. Grier and Price M. Cobbs, is of an influential community leader and his wife, as they attend a therapy session. The wife was borderline suicidal.
>
> She was angry with her husband and berated him for never opening up and exposing his feelings.... The husband remained "nice."...He never raised his

voice above a murmur. His wife could goad him, but he was the epitome of understanding. He was amenable to all suggestions. His manner and gestures were deliberate, studied, and noninflammatory. Everything was understated. During the course of treatment, he was involved in several civil rights crises. His public life was an extension of his private one, and he used such words as "moderation" and "responsibility." His entire life was a study in passivity, in how to play at being a man without really being one.[108]

He made it against all odds. One would wonder how much he had to sacrifice of his identity, his true self, to make a difference. African-Americans, and Black men in particular, have always been compelled to create ways to express themselves to the dominant culture that seem nonthreatening. I heard one such man state that it was "by the grace of God" that he was able to survive, "but it still hurts."

When it comes to powerlessness and rage, the church is not exempt. In the case of pastors and leaders, exposing one's life struggles could cause the congregation to lose confidence, thus weakening the spiritual psyche of the membership or even causing some members to leave the assembly of believers altogether. Church leaders must be cautious in revealing personal struggles to avoid stigmatization. It is all injurious. Overall, wherever there are inequities, the people suffer. Two of the nationally best known and most emblematic instances of the cultural conditioning factor of powerlessness/rage were the death of Dr. Martin Luther King, Jr. in 1968 and the assault on Rodney King in 1991.

From the start, African-Americans could not trust the systems in place to be equitable. Instead, trust in our inherent worth would be the inspiring theme of the civil rights era— "Black power" and "Black is beautiful"—and the songs of encouragement that would uplift our spirits through the years. Do you remember James Brown's "Say It Loud, I'm Black and I'm Proud," Patti LaBelle's "New Attitude," or Whitney Houston's "I'm Every Woman"? All of these hits were happening while the church was singing "We Shall Overcome" and "Lean on Me." Other communally embraced anthems included Nina Simone's "Young, Gifted and Black," Gloria Gaynor's "I Will Survive," Village People's "Macho Man," R. Kelly's "I Believe I Can Fly," Luther Vandross's "Dance with My Father," and Jill Scott's "Golden." Finally yet importantly, Marvin Gaye in "What's Going On" sang a question that is still relevant today.

Twentieth-century America gave rise to the newer refrains of rap and spoken word (language expressed orally) that expressed the belief systems of Gen Xers, Millennials, and Gen Zers. Yet, when I hear these newer songs, I admit I struggle with those lyrics that defame character and denigrate women rather than uplifting hearts. Even more, when I watch mainstream artists who fill stadiums, draw large crowds, and have big followings, but still speak not even a whisper of a word of inspiration, hope, encouragement, and brotherly love for the masses, I wonder what will become of future generations.

The music of the '50s, '60s, and '70s was significant in rebuilding the wounded spirit left by slavery, poverty, and racial inequality. These themes and melodies are the soul of Black folks and became an opportunity for us to accept our uniqueness with pride. Hidden in the lyrics, we found positive affirmations that reflected our true self and praised our value and self-worth to our families and to this nation. We no longer doubted. On the other hand, mass media continued to reinforce negative stereotypes by portraying Blacks as comedians, unintelligent, criminals, lazy, and prone to violence. Sometimes, we found ourselves acting out this same oppressive behavior——we allowed ourselves to suffer role-reversal.

The Willie Lynch theory (as described in chapter 3) intentionally broke down the family structure of the slave. Looking at our struggles today, we wonder if the Willie Lynch approach succeeded.

Additionally, reverse discrimination comes into play against the dominant people group—much like the Bakke decision.[109] For some African-Americans, these responses may appear to be equitable, but they do not soften our burden or remove the pain. When they are held up against the tragedies in our history, we find that today is a good day, but we are aware that, at any moment, another disaster could be hovering on the horizon, and our hope for the future snatched away. As an example, when we tried to make sense of the death of Blacks, both male and female, more violence launched against our communities. In 2012, in Sanford, Florida, George Zimmerman fatally shot Trayvon Martin, and then there was another fatality in August 2014 in Ferguson, Missouri: Michael Brown. Rioting and looting broke out in Ferguson. I was on vacation in New York City when I got the news. I felt the pain. I bowed my head, my heart sank, and I cried out, "Oh! Lord." People in New York, both Black and White, were marching and chanting, "Stop the Killing." That evening we went to church to hear the pastor say that everyone is afraid:

the people, the shop owners, and law enforcement. We need to pray.

Moreover, a new voice took to the streets—Black Lives Matter. Controversial as it may seem, this movement is like a voice crying out in the wilderness, awakening the hearts of African-Americans, bringing awareness to the national consciousness, and allowing African-American voices to be heard. Can we hear the cry? When do we begin to have the conversations to build a strategy for national engagement around social issues that affect our nation because Black Lives Matter, too? (In addition, to the weariness of all, what inevitably followed the Black Lives Matter movement? You got it: White Lives Matter,[110] then there is All Lives Matter.[111] Are we fighting the same battle or not? The answer is NO. America, when are we going to gather and talk about it?

In the face of despair, the Black church continued to be the beacon of hope in the community. Spiritual comfort lies in knowing that we can engage God in a place of community with like-minded souls drawing closer to God. "As for you, you meant evil against me, but God meant it for good" (Genesis 50:20a, NASB). The African-Americans clung to the church's belief system, prayer, praise, worship, and music (the spirituals turn our attention toward the Gospels) to find relief as they continued to sing of their journey on street corners and in nightclubs.

When it comes to rage, we can say that sometimes we only hurt ourselves. Is that not what powerlessness and rage lead to? Rage distorts our sense of balance and our points of view. Sometimes, we have suppressed our feelings for so long that we just do not have the words. Others do not comprehend our pain nor do they recognize a heart spiraling downward with no one to hear our anguish. At times, I wonder if anyone even cares. One such time of discouragement came as we tried to reckon with the tragedy of Ferguson. We were mourning that loss and then, BAM! In June 2015, a lone gunman killed nine people at a midday Bible study at Mother Emanuel AME Church in Charleston, South Carolina. The members of the church chose to do it God's way and forgive. Soon after, the news of "shots fired" in Dallas, Texas, in July 2016, stirred our emotions again. "Police officers down." Families held on for dear life, trying to heal and rediscover a new normal. Tragedy struck again when a man entered the morning service of the Tree of Life Synagogue and killed eleven and injured six, in October 2018, in the Pittsburgh area. The neighborhood was devastated. Yet, in the spirit of goodwill, the Rev. Eric S. C. Manning, senior pastor of Mother Emanuel AME, flew to Pittsburgh to console and to bring words of hope to the members. A dialogue started, reminding us that we must not undervalue the ministry of presence. In moving forward, the Rabbi Jonathan Perlman of Tree of Life is seeking God for the vision of the synagogue so that they can rebuild the brokenness. Yes, rebuild the hearts of the people first.

This is not unlike the story of the freed slave, Charlotte Brooks, which we discussed in chapter 3, who visited her pastor's wife for consolation, hoping to find a companion in her suffering.

We pray there are sacred places, safe places, hospitable places, and nurturing environments for healing to take place. We pray for a spiritual community where those in sorrow and lament can be comforted.

MISTRUST

Our fourth key cultural conditioning factor is *mistrust*, which means "to doubt the truth, validity, or effectiveness of."[112] Despite the history that has already been discussed in this book and the encouraging messages from our families ("you can make it" or "you are somebody"), African-Americans have a merited distrust of the majority culture and its institutions.

From the beginning, African-Americans have seen education as the way out of poverty. Yet, in our society, there were other systems that hindered and gave alarm. In particular, since slavery, Blacks have had to pay attention to the ways they expressed themselves in order to appear nonthreatening to Whites. Fast-forwarding in time, Derald Wing Sue explains that while "segregation of Latino Americans, passage of exclusionary laws against the Chinese, genocide of Native Americans, and internment of Japanese Americans are not in the critical consciousness of most Whites on a day-to-day basis, they have a large-scale impact on the mind-set of people of color."[113] Then, there was the Tuskegee syphilis experiment by the U.S. Public Health Service from 1932 to 1972, an outrageous betrayal of trust still within living memory. For people of color, our consciousness keeps us on alert, and these events are ever before us—thus, the mistrust. This results in a quiet, solemn demeanor, otherwise known as "playing it cool," which is one of the strategies that African-Americans use to "conceal their true thoughts or feelings and appear serene, calm, or non-reactive in the face of racism."[114] To take it a step further, "people of color believed Whites to be deceptive and thus hold biases, prejudices, and stereotypes that they consciously or unconsciously attempt to conceal."[115] Either way, it takes time to decipher what African-Americans call a White code of conduct.

Mistrust, however justified, can lead to further damage by causing African-Americans to reject some helpful practices and institutions. By the mid-to-late 1900s, psychological counseling and therapy became a nationally accepted venue of behavior-based healing therapy for the nation. Initially, African-Americans were reluctant, and there was a resistance to therapy. For those who did solicit help, as time progressed, the questioning style of the counselor or therapist proved intrusive. During the counseling session, the African-American client felt uncomfortable, thus creating an atmosphere of hesitancy and suspicion rather than an amiable safe place of camaraderie and acceptance to explore the inner conflicts of living in America. Alternative methods of small group therapy like Al-Anon emerged in the mid-1900s and continue today. Early on, from a domestic point of view, "many black families perceive therapy to be the process of labeling them as 'crazy.' They often feared the reaction of their extended family members, friends, and community. This is compounded by the fact that black families are often not self-referred but sent for treatment by schools, courts, hospitals, or social welfare agencies, often under considerable threat or pressure."[116] African-Americans continue to face "premature termination, difficulties in racial and ethnic match between client and therapist, *and* psychological misdiagnosis."[117] Lastly, "black therapists, themselves, were...viewed by black families as part of these institutions and thus are not trusted initially."[118] Though therapy is helpful, the Black therapist risks the perception of being part of the system that berates us. The Black therapist must be careful not to propagate the assumptions of an oppressive system as he or she seeks to help members of the community.

MICROAGGRESSIONS: MICRO-ASSAULTS, MICRO-INSULTS, MICRO-INEQUITIES

Even though modern-day African-Americans may not be sensitive to the dynamics of overt racial slurs, there "is an incorporation of such negative images into the personal identity of the black person."[119] Below are two statements, regarding African-Americans, made by members of the ruling class:

> *White male, age 38, newspaperman in Newport News, Virginia:*
> Our colored people are hardworking, self-respecting, and do not attempt to mix anywhere with the whites....The best evidence of the fair treatment they get are the public school facilities. They have very excellent n---- schools.... The Negro is a black and kinky-haired person from whose body comes a not entirely pleasant odor. He is always regarded as an inferior people and race, mentally and morally, destined by birth and circumstances to serve the white people....I do not understand the northerners. How would they like a n---- to marry their daughter?[120]

> *White male, age 25, student in New York City:*
> I have nothing against the blacks, or should I say African-Americans. I go to my classes with them, and we work alongside one another at my office. Okay, I don't socialize with them much outside of class, but they keep to

themselves anyway. There is nothing wrong with being with people who share your interests. Frankly, I don't like rap music, and I'm not sure it's really music anyway.... Please don't misunderstand me, if they like it, that's fine. Interracial relationships are fine. I don't object. But, I do worry about the children, though. It's going to be hard on them...being mixed.[121]

As years have progressed, overt statements like these have lessened, but their spiritual impact has not. Statements such as the ones above continue to hit a raw nerve in the souls of African-Americans and still reinforce a sense of powerlessness. Today, these softened overtones have produced a different categorical term, namely, *microaggressions*, which are "brief, everyday exchanges that send denigrating messages to a target group, such as people of color; religious minorities, women, people with disabilities, and gay, lesbian, bisexual, and transgendered individuals."[122]

There are three different types of microaggressions: micro-assaults, micro-insults, and micro-inequities. For African-Americans, micro-assaults (conscious) are "deliberate biased attitudes, beliefs, or behaviors that are communicated to marginalized groups...through verbalization or behaviors... to attack the group identity or to hurt/harm the intended victim through name-calling, avoidant behavior, or purposeful discriminatory actions."[123] This blatant racism is easy to deal with as compared to the second, more subtle type of microaggression: micro-insults.

Micro-insults (unconscious) "convey stereotypes, rudeness, and insensitivity...that demean a person's racial, gender, or sexual orientation, heritage, or identity."[124]

An example of this phenomenon took place in Texas in 2016, and it involved a White couple and an African-American female shopping in the grocery store. A young police officer's spouse had left church and gone grocery shopping when a White couple noticed her car and stylish attire. The man and his wife approached her and asked what she did for a living. The police officer's wife refused to respond and continued her shopping, yet the White couple stalked her and abruptly insisted that she answer their question ("You mean you are not going to answer my question?"). This time the young wife acknowledged that she was a beautician and her husband worked hard as a police officer. The overt insult to this beautician could be a provocation to anger—"Here we go again." Nevertheless, she answered because she felt that the couple was looking to hear that she was a drug pusher or some other kind of a derelict—another negative assumption that would add to a deprived mindset. She felt that by responding, the White couple would have something positive to say about African-Americans when they spoke with their friends—or would they?

I applaud the beautician's response; still there is something inside of me that doubts the intention of the White couple. I confess to doubt. Even I, as an African-American Christian, face awkward moments like these and life becomes tedious and wearisome.

Third, micro-inequities (unconscious) "describe the pattern of being overlooked, under-respected, and devalued because of one's race or gender...they are often unconsciously delivered as subtle snubs or dismissive looks, gestures, and tones."[125] For African-Americans, our relationship with the Lord and identity in Christ become the keys to freedom, even through the scars and ill-treatment.

Because we have been accepted and affirmed in Christ, this freedom should fuel within us a passion to love even the unlovable. With confidence, compassion, and a desire to dismantle stereotypical thinking, we are able to respond more constructively to these microaggressions of life and to society as a whole. Hence, we can view those tainted messages through the eyes of love as opportunities to inform and enlighten others. "Be reconciled to God" (2 Corinthians 5:20b, NRSV).

These random statements and perceived messages listed on page 120 from Derald Wing Sue are examples of a few common microaggressions confronted by people of color. The first column contains the themes of the microaggression. The second column states the actual words of the microaggression, and the third column contains the message that people of color receive when they hear these statements. Even I have been guilty of a few of these statements until I learned better. I am still working on this in my life. Take a look at the chart on the next page.

When we look at a portion of the discussion that involves White privilege, defined as "the unearned benefits and advantages that automatically accrue to Whites by virtue of their skin color,"[126] we understand that it owes its existence to White supremacy. When we look at the other side of the coin, White privilege "automatically disempowers and oppresses people of color."[127] One may have avoided involvement in the historic events of injustices in this nation, even as part of the dominant culture. Yet despite one's actions or inactions, in reality, as members of the majority ruling class, White people have benefitted from these wrongs. However, we will find a few who are sensitive to the times in which we live. They want to do the

Examples of Racial and Gender Microaggressions[128]

Theme	Microaggression	Message
Alien in Their Own Land When we assume Asian Americans and Latino Americans are foreign-born.	"Where are you from?" "Where were you born?" "You speak English very well."	You are not American.
	A person asking an Asian American to teach them words in their native language.	You are a foreigner.
Ascription of Intelligence Assigning intelligence to a person of color or a woman based on their race/gender.	"You are a credit to your race."	People of color are generally not as intelligent as Whites.
	"Wow! How did you become so good at math?"	It is unusual for a woman to be smart in math.
	Asking an Asian person to help with a math or science problem.	All Asians are intelligent and good in math and sciences.
Color Blindness Statements that indicate a White person does not want to acknowledge race.	When I look at you I don't see color.	Denying a person of color's racial/ethnic experiences.
	America is a Melting Pot.	Assimilate/acculturate to dominant culture.
	There is only one race, the human race.	The individual is denied as a racial/cultural being.
Criminality/Assumption of Criminal Status We presume a person of color to be dangerous, a criminal, or a deviant based on their race.	A White man or woman clutches their purse or checks their wallet as a Black or Latino approaches or passes.	You are a criminal.
	A storeowner follows a customer of color around the store.	You are going to steal. You are poor. You do not belong.
	A White person waits to ride the next elevator when a person of color is on it.	You are dangerous.

Theme	Microaggression	Message
Denial of Individual Racism/Sexism/ Heterosexism A statement made when bias is denied.	"I'm not racist. I have several Black friends."	I am immune to racism because I have friends of color.
	"As an employer, I always treat men and women equally."	I am incapable of sexism.
Pathologizing Cultural Values/Communication Styles The notion that the values and communication styles of the dominant/White culture are ideal.	Asking a Black person, "Why do you have to be so loud? Just calm down."	Assimilate to dominant culture.
	To an Asian or Latino person, "Why are you so quiet? We want to know what you think. Be more verbal. Speak up more."	
	Dismissing an individual who brings up race/culture in work/school setting.	Leave your cultural baggage outside.
Second Class Citizen Occurs when a target group member receives differental treatment from the power group.	A person of color is mistaken for a service worker.	People of color are servants to Whites. They could not possibly occupy high status positions.
	A female doctor is mistaken for a nurse.	Women ccoupy nurturing roles.
	A taxicab passes a person of color to pick up a White passsenger.	You are likely to cause trouble and/or travel to a dangerous neighborhood.
	Ignoring a person of color at a store counter to give attention to a White customer behind them.	Whites are more valued customers than people of color.

right thing and put love in action. Nevertheless, often they still pay a high price for their allegiance to honor and integrity.

A close friend relayed this story about a White family living in Washington, DC, who marched with Dr. Martin Luther King, Jr. back in the day. Even parents are tested when raising their children—let's listen in.

Their teenage daughter came home one afternoon after playing with the kids on the block because the family down the street invited her to join them at the Glen Echo amusement park on the upcoming Saturday afternoon. When she asked for permission from her parents, they said "no" and told her to tell the family that she would not be able to go to Glen Echo Park until it becomes integrated and all people can go. Without a hesitation, a jest, an outburst of anger, or a threat, she walked out of the house to relay to the family down the street her parents' wishes. She trusted that her parents had her best interest at heart and did not complain. Glen Echo Park integrated in 1961.

I spoke with the daughter, who remembers having conversations about race around the dining room table with her mother and schoolmates. She is a grandmother now. She still reads and she still has the conversations. This is a question for everyone: What impact are we having on our children and on the next generation?

Here is another example of White privilege that I encountered in my own life. To understand it, you must keep in mind the context: because of the power structures in our country, the White person, here, has the capacity to consider multiple options when he or she faces a life decision. The African-American has far fewer options available to him or her.

It was 1996; a meeting was taking place at a big aerospace company facing layoffs. I was in the meeting when I heard the voice of a White, middle-aged woman say that she would be willing to give up her position voluntarily. I knew this woman, and I was shocked. After the meeting, I asked her why, as a manager, she would volunteer for a layoff when she was more than qualified for the work she was doing in her division. She simply said that she was well off and that her family did not need her salary.

For her, being laid off was not a problem; for me the fear of being unemployed was staggering, and I felt powerless. Even if laid off, as a member of the dominant culture, she still had the assurance that she *was employable*. "I can always get a job" was her underlying assumption.

Now, there is nothing wrong with that assumption or statement, but we must simply acknowledge the truth that this inward belief reflects to her White privilege. Even though she tried to encourage me by turning to me and telling me that I would be fine, her encouragement did not take into account the realities of my situation. It did not take into account *my* journey and the pitfalls of *my* cultural experience.

Next, let us look at an impromptu conversation—a sensitive time of sharing as a young African-American police officer recounts a conversation with a retired White police captain that happened in a restaurant. For some this may seem like two officers simply chatting as the senior officer related a story to the young officer. A closer look will reveal underlying spiritual implications. This conversation took place shortly after the death of Trayvon Martin.

The ex-police captain approached a young African-American officer when he was dressed in uniform and having dinner with his wife. The young officer acknowledged the ex-police captain, and they stepped off to the side as the captain shared a pivotal experience of his: an African-American man had filed a complaint for harassment against one of the White officers in his division. When approached by the captain, the White officer admitted that he had stopped the African-American male because he was driving a nice car and the officer wanted to know how he could afford such a vehicle. During the captain's investigation, he uncovered that this officer had a history of stopping African-Americans without cause and that the officer's father was a high-ranking member of the Ku Klux Klan. Emotions heightened during the captain's investigation and led to internal conflicts and skirmishes within the division. At the end of the investigation, the captain submitted his report, and the officer was discharged.

Afterward, havoc broke out within the division against the captain, who had honored his pledge to enforce the law, done his homework, and presented the facts of the investigation. He now was under attack. He loved the job, but the vocation forced him into early retirement. Strangely, the conversation took a shift as the captain discussed with the officer the ire of White Americans when they see African-Americans dominating sports and drawing large salaries. I wonder what other issues caused the White privileged in America to struggle as it pertains to African-American achievements and investments in this society. The lens focuses upon the inequity of the judicial system during this time. Nonetheless, the retired police captain ended his conversation with a word of caution and encouragement to the young police officer; the captain believed that becoming a peace officer is an honorable and noble profession and told the peace officer to "hang in there."

It is important that the White captain and the Black officer together had the conversation. The underlying spiritual issue was the true focus. The captain desired to encourage the young officer in a vocation that he was still passionate about, even after it had mistreated him. He wanted to let the officer know that he was not alone.

Issues around law enforcement are a sensitive topic. At the time of this writing, the statistics of African-Americans enrolling into the police academy overall are on the decline. This is not good for our culture or society as a whole. If we are not at the table, who will speak for us? This exchange between the officer and the captain is an example of having the conversation in a safe space, where feelings are shared honestly. At times, it seems that we are damned if we do and damned if we don't. In reality, there can be negative consequences when we do what is right and fair. What emotion(s) does this conversation stir up in you? I believe that these impromptu conversations are happening all over this nation, which is good, but it is not enough. How can we keep this dialogue going?

The goal of having the conversation is to reveal the deeper spiritual issues of our lives. Recognizing the incidents of micro-assaults, micro-insults, and micro-inequities are important, but more important are the spiritual issues—our motives and the intents of our hearts. The conversation helps us to find ways to discover the truth within, and these truths will transform our lives. I am hopeful that as Christians we can become greater vessels for change in this society.

IMPACT OF THE RECESSION

In 2007, society overall, including special interest groups, the poor, the underprivileged, and the disabled, had benefitted from the economic upturn. Things seemed to be going well. Then, suddenly—*CRASH!* The bottom fell out, and we were in a recession. Many people's lifestyles, including those of African-Americans, plummeted. Again, all forms of microaggression surged against African-Americans and people of color, resulting in an unemployment rate that catapulted to an all-time high.[129] See the graph below for an overall view of unemployment over the last twenty years.

Unemployment Rates by Race and Hispanic or Latino Ethnicity 1973—2016[130]

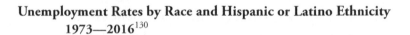

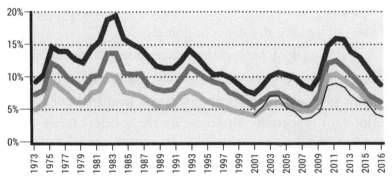

Lost jobs translated into lost wages, loss of homes, and no place to go for assistance. The now-resurging economy might indicate that we have recovered, but countless of our brothers and sisters of color remain unemployed, and those searching for jobs often do not get a call back. Some available jobs render them unable to sustain even the basic necessities of life. The dominant culture will say, "We are only trying to feed our families," and that is probably true. Moreover, I say to the marketplace and believers alike, "So are we." This is Christendom. Yet, many of today's African-Americans still struggle to make ends meet, often unable to rise above mediocrity.

Hope diminishes in our children as they grow up believing they will not be better off than their parents. The costs of living and education skyrocket, and they end up in jobs for which they are overqualified. You would not believe the number of college graduates working at Starbucks and McDonald's. That being the case, how do we prepare future generations to address the blatant and subtle innuendos of other ethnic groups, including Whites, and illuminate truth without minimizing our integrity? The Eurocentric worldview of individualism continues to separate us and penetrate throughout the very fiber of this great nation. Millennials and Generation Xers raise important questions that we in Christendom struggle to answer to their satisfaction. We cannot put old wine into new wine skins.

AFRICAN-AMERICAN LIBERATION

Now, more African-Americans are taking advantage of one-on-one counseling to improve behavior and cognitive skills that aid in addressing experiences, the past, the present, and other socioeconomic realities.

Earlier I spoke of an African-American view of the African-American therapist. A look at the point of view of the White therapist offers a different conclusion. It was noted that the "white clinicians interviewed saw the differences between black and white families as related solely to class and not to racial differences....It is easier and more comfortable to deny that racial differences exist and to see problems only in class or economic terms."[131] Sue, in his summary statements in *Micro-aggressions in Everyday Life*, encourages African-Americans to understand the "modern form of racism that operates in such a manner as to preserve the non-prejudiced self-image of whites by offering them convenient rationalizations for their actions; they are prevented from recognizing their own racial biases or the implicit prejudicial attitudes they harbor toward others."[132]

The dominant culture has relied on the judgments of their parents and community. They were deceived as was the young nine-year-old taught by Miss Helen. The generational implications carried forth in the status quo are that "such a form of self-deception is reinforced by: (a) racism as a sickness and does not exist in good and decent human beings, (b) racism is only associated with dramatic, overt hate crimes, and (c) good citizens do not engage in such heinous acts."[133] I believe that recognizing this deception and drawing upon a psychological balance may not resolve the issue, but it will aid in our ability to properly investigate and

128

address inappropriate behavior and hurtful statements. This, subsequently, opens the door for spiritual engagements that reinforce deeper self-truths from God's perspective. In doing so, African-Americans bring balance to the situation when we are able to acknowledge that the unconstructive self-images and identity projections are untrue in God's eyes. When we look at ourselves from God's perspective, we are accepted and affirmed. That is who we are. When we overshadow our internal scars with love, I believe our hearts will soften, and we will see that the overt or covert behavior of the dominant culture is a cry for help, too.

For families, self-care is vital, whether that care is through a spiritual guide, mentor, coach, or therapist. Any of these self-help agents can begin to "mobilize the family's ability to successfully interact with external systems."[134] Therapy can bring empowerment and encouragement, but how does one offset the devastation of not only the legacy of slavery but also ongoing oppression from within the ranks of society in general? Many attempts have been employed by social scientists and educators to define a process of minority identification; however, the "most influential is the Cross model[135] of psychological nigrescence (the process of becoming black)."[136] Developed during the Civil Rights movement, this model delineates a five-stage process in which Blacks in the United States move from a White frame of reference to a positive Black frame of reference. Whether or not the therapist used this model, the therapist can no longer generalize. This type of therapy changes the therapist as well in that it "forces the therapist to examine his or her own values and political, cultural, religious beliefs and biases, and to intervene accordingly."[137]

CLOSING THOUGHTS

Finally, the class and value system struggles are a daily nemesis. The African-American must be aware that long-term exposure to perceived racism has physiological and psychological
consequences. Holding on to one's identity and heritage while
defending against overt and subtle racial slurs and misrepre-
sentations is exhausting. Is there no end? Sue acknowledges
that "microaggression depletes the psychological and spiritual
energies that distract from listening and learning, working at
maximum efficiency...and dealing with the daily routines of
life."[138] Whether overt or subtle, "whites may be perceived as
symbols of racism whether it's intentionally or innocently....
As a result, blacks may approach interracial interactions with
a great deal of suspicion and guardedness, may not readily disclose their true thoughts and feelings...to discern the motives
of others."[139] At the end of the day, "there is one overmastering
problem that the socially and politically disinherited always
face: How then do African-Americans 'sing the songs of Zion'
in this barren land? Under what terms is survival possible?"[140]
More than individual survival is at stake. In spite of microaggressions, this generation of African-Americans must learn
our history and take responsibility to educate themselves. We
must become reconciling voices to other ethnic groups, while
simultaneously engaging social justice issues at large. For we do
not stand alone.

SIX LET'S TAKE A CLOSER LOOK

In this chapter, we talked about how "class and value system struggles are a daily nemesis." Nevertheless, scars can heal. When we come together to discuss our differences and expectations, we learn and we grow.

1. Was there anything presented in this chapter that you are having a hard time believing? If so, it would be worth rehearsing.

2. Since you have been reading, where do you sense feelings of indifference? Where are these feelings coming from?

3. Under these conditions, how do you sense feelings of love and empathy?

4. Consider your struggles and longings as pointing toward a greater potential to live in the fullness of God's purpose for your life. Maybe this would be a good time to journal your thoughts.

SEVEN

Spiritual Formation and Reclaiming Our Community

Of the sons of Issachar, men who understood the times, with knowledge of what Israel should do.

—1 CHRONICLES 12:32A, NASB

And He summoned the crowd with His disciples, and said to them, "If anyone wishes to come after Me, he must deny himself, and take up his cross and follow Me."

—MARK 8:34, NASB

WE HAVE CLOSELY examined the history of African-Americans in the United States and seen the effects of history on the larger culture, on African-American culture, and on the psyche of African-Americans.

In order to begin this chapter with hope, I want to quote a story here that provides an example of how the Black church has historically worked together in community:

In May 1854, [a slave named] Pembrook fled with his two sons, Robert and Jacob. They made it to New York City, where they had family, including Pembrook's brother, a pastor of an African

American Presbyterian church. Once the escape was determined, New York City issued an arrest warrant. Eventually, all three were apprehended in New York and arrested as fugitives....The petitions in the case state that Pembrook...had been enslaved for more than 18 years to Jacob H. Grove....After a short hearing, and based on depositions of Grove and a few others, the court decided that Stephen Pembrook and his sons should be returned to Jacob H. Grove and taken back to Maryland. This story is particularly interesting in the way Stephen Pembrook later regained his freedom. His brother's church, through the donations of parishioners, purchased him for $1,000 and brought him back to New York. His sons, unfortunately, remained in slavery.[141]

As mentioned earlier, much of this generation of African-Americans does not know our history; stories like this one become important. We must remember how we have worked together in the past, in order to keep alive our determination to work together in the days ahead.

Now it is time to turn from problems to look at some solutions: specifically, solutions that only the church can offer—the church as an entity and/or the church individually.

With the changing trends in society, the need for collaboration is even more crucial if we are to fulfill God's call to love—that is, to fulfill the Great Commission.[142] This mandate contains the promise of Christ to be with us on this journey. No one is exempt; all are included—men, women, and children. If we are to build this bridge and fulfill our role as ambassadors for Christ, it starts now. We are going to focus on two solutions. The first is the discipleship model of Spiritual Formation, which is a Eurocentric spiritual concept. In looking at this model, we will also examine how the African-American's cultural perspective can offer something deeper and more community focused. The second solution is reclaiming our community—the idea of taking back the parts of our African heritage lost over the years or minimized and/or denigrated by the majority culture. With this inclusivity and with our focus on love and unity, we can become a catalyst for change in the church universal.

SPIRITUAL FORMATION

As we shared earlier, Spiritual Formation is a means of grace "through which God conforms us to the image of Christ for the sake of others."[143] This is the gift of the Holy Spirit. Embedded within Spiritual Formation are spiritual disciplines or practices. These spiritual practices were my friends during this writing and are the method that I will continue to use to discern kingdom pursuits and reconciliation that extend beyond my native prerogatives.

When I began the project of writing this book and before I was clear on how to proceed, I went to my garage and picked up books that had been on the shelf for almost twenty years. As I think through my time at Biola's Institute for Spiritual Formation (ISF), I can see that the experience was critical to my overall spiritual development. The readings, the prayer projects, and the retreats, as well as class time, were instrumental in the healing process. Whether we attend school, some other training, or we just love the Word of God, even more important are the relationships that we form and the felt sense of community. At ISF, this formula was an opportunity to find my identity in Christ and to learn of God's faithfulness and love. I felt accepted and loved. Yet, I knew my journey would be different. In preparation for this writing, though painful at times, I was able to read the scholarly material, which included a rehearsal of the slave narratives, with a fresh eye of hope. As I read and meditated, my prayer was "Lord, what would you have me to learn from this experience?"

As we noted in chapter 2, Western culture sees Spiritual Formation and soul care as processes with a primary goal of transforming the individual Christian into the likeness of Christ. Similar disciplines indwelled the lifestyles of indigenous African people—disciplines of prayer, praise, and worship. These core disciplines strengthen the community as a whole. Going forward in this chapter, as we examine the role of Spiritual Formation in addressing the cultural conditioning factors present in modern African-American life, we will keep that whole-community focus in mind.

As Christian believers, we must ask ourselves, are we willing to live "independent of God, apart from his love, and beyond the reach of his will"?[144] Whatever the circumstances, the Body of Christ has a choice. With spiritual practices, we can dig into the trenches to transform our families and our communities, to bring about a sense of unity, and to make a greater impact in the kingdom. What is our heart's desire? We have the arsenal. The question becomes, will we dig into the trenches together to bring about a transformation in our personal lives and to be a catalyst for change in the lives of our families, our community, or our churches? Can we bring about a sense of unity for a greater impact in the kingdom? This is a question for everyone. Will we remain in our silos? Remember that separate does not mean equal.

The focus of Spiritual Formation is not on solving problems but on the Problem Solver—namely, the person of the Holy Spirit. These practices do not rely on behavior modification. Instead, they seek to address the core of the inner life of the heart where transformation takes place. Spiritual Formation is designed to "aid Christians in their spiritual growth.... [It] involves learning to discern God's will and the leading of God's Spirit....It is more oriented to a deepening faith and an increasing awareness of the presence of God."[145] That gives us power to fight the deceptions of the enemy, who would tell us to work harder, do more, and also resist the longings of the flesh to be in control. This means we must develop a more intimate relationship with God and with Jesus, God's Son. This is Christ's invitation. Here the exercise and practice of the spiritual disciplines are important because we were not meant to journey alone. When we look to the African-American community, the common tools of Spiritual Formation that we find (in addition to a strong sense of community) are the disciplines of the study of the Word of God, prayer, praise, and worship. Aside from therapy, other discipleship methods for Spiritual Formation—which include retreats, exercises in detachment (relinquishing control), truth-telling, solitude and silence, and seeking out Christian spiritual guides or spiritual mentors in a one-on-one setting—would constitute a relatively new approach in most African-American churches. Today, many African-American churches focus on discipleship, which may consist of an in-house ministry or counseling center as a means of providing long-term solutions for the everyday problems of life and living. Another group exists—those in our congregation who are concerned about their relationship with the Lord. Where do they fit?

Mentoring is a buzzword, whereas *Christian spiritual guides or companions* are terms that have a deeper meaning and represent an inward spiritual approach to issues concerning the heart and conforming to the likeness of Christ. This is pivotal for God's beloved people on their faith journeys. When we incorporate spiritual practices as part of a daily rhythm of life, certain internal, disguised behaviors come to the light. By having these conversations, now we all can explore the deceptive devices of our hearts. We will find that many of them are of our own doing but that many others are the tricks and schemes of the enemy to keep the Body of Christ trapped. By not talking to one another, we remain alone and afraid. By having the conversations that our spiritual growth requires, we are on the road to enlightenment, to recovery, and this new healthiness spills over into our churches. How will the Body of Christ respond to the inner truth within our souls? Have we forgotten that we are Christ's ambassadors?

A robust approach to ministry that meets the needs of the congregation is needed. When we touch on social justice issues, address diversity, and discuss societal influences in a way that promotes inclusion, the world will be affected. Everybody has a story. In reality, we are not the America we used to be. That being the case, we are not the church we used to be either.

All believers possess the gift of the Holy Spirit and the biblical mandates of the Great Commandment and the Great Commission. If we are to fulfill God's will and purpose on this earth, the church must grapple with the following questions:

How do we relate to the Holy Spirit and participate with the work of the Holy Spirit in a society that appears to have turned its back on God and the church?

How does the church measure spiritual growth and transformation where love is the defining marker? "You will know them by their fruits" (Matthew 7:16a, NRSV).

How does the church tap into critical skills, talents, and gifts of the membership to build disciples, evangelize the community, and bridge the gap left by woundedness, distrust, apathy, and disinterest?

Psychologically, as we engage the tenets of the "love one another" commandment of Jesus and take seriously the spiritual disciplines, we will find that more and more African-Americans are changing their perceptions and seeking help. They are seeing the advantages of Christian-based self-help opportunities through counseling, inner healing, deliverance ministries, spiritual guides, mentoring, and coaching. Whether we are trained or untrained, schooled or unschooled, male or female, slave or free, God is able to uniquely orchestrate the lives of His people to receive the totality of His love in whatever state they exist and to help them produce the fruits of righteousness.

The cultural conditioning factors described earlier are a hindrance to the advancement of the Gospel of Jesus Christ specifically and African-Americans overall. Now the victim becomes the perpetrator with messages of hope cloaked in unresolved pain and suffering. The result is religious stagnation, except for the intentional few who are passionate about their relationship with the Lord. This book was never intended to provide every single answer to the African-American's personal dilemma, but I hope to open minds to alternative approaches toward spiritual growth—approaches that will result in a community that unifies us. The good news is that everyone has a place at the table and a part in the great kingdom work. For "God is no respecter of persons" (Acts 10:34b, KJV). As members of the body of a believing community, the church, the saints in the believing community must be intentional. The question is not what, but how and when.

RECLAIMING OUR TRADITIONS: COMMUNITY

The church universal is separated more than ever. Millennials and Gen Xers have little knowledge of how previous generations "hoped against hope," yet, though they may ignore it, they carry the DNA of our journey of racism and segregation within. Can you hear the cry for help? Wake up, children! A community mindset within our culture sustains our belief system. To bridge the generational gap that separates us requires the following: (1) time with the Father, and (2) continuing the ongoing work of sanctification. We must unveil the truth of a seared consciousness, confess our sins, and receive our healing. Somewhere along the line, we as African-Americans will begin the conversation with White America, with people of color, with youth, with our peers, and prayerfully move toward a common ground to promote unity. (We will talk more about this conversation in the next chapter.)

This study of the journey of the relational aspects of African-Americans in this nation has raised several topics for consideration for all believers if we, overall, are to become healthy, mature Christians, functioning within God's kingdom agenda.

Foundational to the dynamics of the African-American church are the Word of God, prayer, praise, music, and community. African-Americans should know their history and learn to love its rich heritage. Our contributions are chronicled in the biblical narrative from Genesis when God "formed man from the dust of the ground, and breathed into his nostrils the breath of life; and the man became a living being" (Genesis 2:7, NRSV) to the book of Revelation. This book describes a "great multitude that no one could count, from every nation, from all tribes and peoples and languages, standing before the throne and before the Lamb" (Revelation 7:9a, NRSV). The African-American contributions to this nation are endless, and this legacy should be an ongoing refrain to succeeding generations throughout their lives.

How does one get African-American communities to embrace their rich legacy in this country and to share it with the succeeding generations? The believer and believing church should consider long-term approaches that capitalize on the African-American psyche and cultural dynamics, while also addressing any cultural conditioning factors. There exists the need to break through the false self that looms as a veil over our identity in Christ, clouds our thinking on social justice and our freedom. It is in sacred space and time, through grace, that the Spirit rebuilds the inner self in Christ. Programs and events have yet to produce the spiritual fruit of true righteousness and discipleship. We actualize our potential and destiny through our cooperation with the Spirit's work.

How can the believing community at-large better equip themselves to develop long-term approaches that penetrate and break through the daunting silence of the false self and rebuild the inner self in truth, freedom, and love? Shepherding is a means of nurturing and soul care that entrusts the heart to God. "The LORD is my shepherd,...He makes me lie down in green pastures;...he restores my soul" (Psalm 23:1a, 2a, 3a, NRSV). Though the core spiritual practices of prayer, study of the Word of God, praise, and worship are the mainstays of the church, many church members and their leaders are suffering from burnout, isolation, and discouragement. They have found that their ministry life has drifted into a mess of busywork. Projects and programs become the norm in the hope of attracting the unsaved, the backslider, and the coming generations. Still, church attendance is declining.

How and when will we learn to slow down and be with the Lord in timeless stillness for our own personal well-being and the refreshing of our own souls, which prepare us for the work ahead? We must expand our spiritual rhythm of life to incorporate alternative means of grace (the Word of God, contemplative prayer, silence, etc.) that focus on intimacy with God. Our God is a God of relationships, who will enable us to carry the torch to the future. By engaging these timeless spiritual practices to shine the light of love on these tender, sensitive places at our core, we learn to trust the eternal God to heal the blemishes of the past. We are energized, and our hearts are stirred for the kingdom work ahead. Christian spirituality is more than just going to church on Sunday.

HEALING RELATIONSHIPS WITHIN THE COMMUNITY OF THE CHURCH

How can African-Americans and their churches embrace alternate means of grace that speak to the depths of our hearts on one hand and on the other invoke the power of God to make a response to this great Gospel?

In our historical reflections within this book, we have identified the African-American church as the center for religious, social, and political activity, and for spiritual renewal. We discussed the four cultural conditioning factors that African-Americans face—sacred secrets, identity, powerlessness/rage, and mistrust—from three viewpoints: historically, culturally, and psychologically. Let us seize this Kairos moment in time as Dr. Martin Luther King, Jr.'s prophetic voice comes to fruition. Remember that we bore witness to the first president of color, President Barack Obama. For African-Americans, this keeps hope alive in the hearts of God's people and the church, and it lets us know that God sees us. As for me, the lyrics of the song "We've Come This Far by Faith" come to mind:

> We've come this far by faith, leaning on the Lord;
> Trusting in His Holy Word, He's never failed me yet.
> Oh, oh—, oh—can't turn around—
> We've come this far by faith.[146]

Today, many uninformed people have said the church "does not play as crucial a role in providing for emotional support as do family and friends."[147] The historical issues that plague the church universal did not leave the African-American church unscarred after the Civil War. Both African-American and non-African-American churches were ill equipped to address the needs of the people in a growing population in this nation. The African-American church almost collapsed under the strain of "anti-clericalism, secularism, and nihilism in the black urban communities of the North."[148] The churches that survived, as suggested in the book *Embodied Spirits: Stories of Spiritual Directors of Color*, had a "positive sense of God and God's presence in their lives. They...knew that 'God is able' to bring them through their problems, that God can...heal and deliver them from their devastating circumstances, and would never abandon them in their times of trouble and misfortune."[149]

African-Americans consciously and unconsciously drew from the unfathomable spiritual resilience of their ancestors, who struggled with—and yet survived—the evils of slavery, Jim Crow laws, segregation, and contemporary disenfranchisement (exclusion/marginalization); in other words, they showed "hope against hope." They maintained much of the African heritage of praise, musical worship, and community, which remain the cornerstone and signature of the African-American church. With the community consciousness so ingrained in their hearts, they protected their loved ones, nurtured the young, and cared for widows. We gathered at mealtimes, shared our stories, supported our families, and educated our children. Traditional values associated with family celebrations of births, marriages, and deaths, as well as respect for authority and for the wisdom of the elder members became ceremonial celebrations. Then, there are the Black Family Reunions that pass our historical legacy from one generation to another.

Community held the Black church together until more opportunities appeared, with big business and merchants opening their doors in the Industrial Revolution, and then World War II providing much-needed jobs. Soon after that, the educational systems of the local schools and seminaries widened their policies for admission. Slowly, we entered the revolving door of progress, but the door of equality remained closed in many cases, while the door of our hearts remained guarded.

Jesus is still calling, "Come to Me."

The words of Howard Thurman's grandmother come to mind. He remembered her saying, "You are not slaves. You are not n-----. You're God's children!"[150] These words echoed to him as an adult whenever he faced the crossroads of life. For him, these words "established...the ground of personal dignity."[151] For African-American Christians, "Who I am?" is a question of identity that begs an answer.

So, I ask again: How do African-Americans define themselves? Do African-Americans define themselves in terms of roles, such as by job, by marital status, by gender, by family, by culture, by accomplishment, by racial identity? Who are we, really? Are African-Americans to be defined by their circumstances in life or by the church they attend?

Initially, the slaveholders and slave owners defined the Africans with terms such as "n-----," "darkie," or "colored." Post–Civil War emancipation enabled the freedmen to reject negative opinions and redefine their self-worth in ways detached from the chains of this world. Racial integrity replaced racial socialization, and the identity "Black" emerged. Is that the African-American Christian's identity? When Afrocentricity, designed to "promote emphasis on African culture and the contributions of Africans to the development of Western civilization,"[152] evolved, "Black" became "African-American," but who are African-American Christians, really? "Even though a man may be convinced of his infinite worth as a child of God, the environment may not in itself give him the opportunity for self-realization and fulfillment that his Spirit demands."[153] More often than not, the African-American church responded to the questions "What am I?" or "What must I do?" in the form of liberation theology that focuses on the social justice issues of the times.

In actuality, the African-American church became the platform to provide role models and mentors for both young and older members. By modeling godliness, the church fathers, church mothers, and other mature believers were and still are major contributors to the legacy of our race. They are vital in shaping lives and building character and self-esteem in this generation so that those who come after them can take their rightful place in society. The use of the gifts and talents of African-Americans denied by White evangelicalism, corporate America, and society as a whole are identified, developed, and reaffirmed in the Black church and in family life. Alongside the preached word, which serves as a witness of God and God's liberating activity in history, other relational-focused ministries within the African-American church community are doing important work. These include, as we have said, the study of the Word of God, discipleship training, mentoring, and revivals. There are also special programs and events that reinforce the need for fellowship and spiritual growth.

Sensitive to our plight, even pastors and church leaders must be cautious with the people over whom the Lord has given them oversight. This unique relationship between pastor and people is one of respect, compassion, love, and esteem, and it finds its roots in the African sense of community. During slavery, the evangelists/exhorters risked their lives to bring the Lord's message of truth to the enslaved. Often, the preacher himself was a slave who resided among them and worked alongside them. He was the one beaten and scourged. In those days, the parishioners had great respect for their pastors, and this tradition has carried on down throughout the generations. Today, we know more and understand more. This same bond between pastor and people exists today. If we are not careful, it can lead to blind devotion that allows the pastor to act autonomously. They could use the leadership and trustee boards as rubber stamps for ministry decisions that are not Spirit-led and could have negative impacts on the membership at-large. Without a system of spiritual accountability and without exercising checks and balances, how can God's plan move forward? Further, how does a pastor promote stewardship, integrity, and godliness within the congregation?

Sometimes, the pressures of the pulpit can be overwhelming. Many pastors and leaders walk this vocation alone in isolation and abandonment, feeling trapped. Meetings and the business of the church consume our church leaders. Some experience burnout; others become power-hungry and abusive. They find few that understand their plight, and fewer still that can be trusted. The results of this perceived chasm are that the family is at risk and ministry is at risk, and these hinder kingdom work. Eventually, the question becomes the same as the one Jesus offered to the man at the pool of Bethesda: "Do you wish to get well?" (John 5:6c, NASB). We need renewal and refreshment. If we are not careful, instead of seeking retreat and healing, we will simply escape, not knowing how to care for our souls or how to draw upon the streams of living water for rest and restoration. We cannot work in isolation.

The phrases "care of souls" or "soul care," as mentioned earlier, can both be defined as "a practice of aiding another to mature and be formed in the Christian life."[154] Soul care becomes a place where one does not have to walk this journey of faith alone. Central to our church message are these core basic concepts and practices, namely, the Word of God, prayer, praise, and worship. However, there has been less focus on other spiritual practices, like retreat, silence and solitude, Christian spiritual guides, and *lectio divina* to name a few. These contemplative practices foster intimacy with God. "For out of the abundance of the heart the mouth speaketh" (Matthew 12:34b, KJV). The African-American church often does not recognize these spiritual practices. However, we can rest in the fact that God used the innate natural tendencies of the African-American community to nurture, sustain, and mature the people of faith. We can rest there, even as we move on to new methods of spiritual maturity and growth. For it is within community, only when the people of God "stand with those who suffer pain, humiliation, starvation, and poverty and look at the world through their experience will we truly know the God who came into the world to share human pain [*and who died for our sins*]....If we run from pain in ourselves and others, we will never know [intimacy], peace or joy with any real depth."[155]

Through an understanding of our identity in Christ, we are able to see through the mask of privilege and misguidedness. We are capable of overcoming the cultural conditioning factors of sacred secrets, powerlessness/rage, and mistrust through the experience of finding our true selves in God's love. Believe me, God does use our experiences and the relationships of others (spiritual friends and companions). If African-Americans are to reclaim our authentic selves, "we must go back and reclaim our historic past so we can move forward, so we understand why and how we came to be who we are today."[156] This prepares us to fulfill our destiny through the mission that calls us. By maintaining our relationship with the heavenly Father and others, we sustain and heal the tortured soul. It is through suffering that we learn the love of self and love of neighbor.

OVERCOMING HISTORY

In spite of the prevailing religious teaching throughout American society, the uneducated slaves were able to look past the fallibility of doctrinal error and perceive the truth of God's Word. They endured the painful schemes of their oppressors as well as the religious instructions of a mangled Gospel bent toward their psychological destruction. These left invisible wounds, the scars that remain, affecting the slave's ability to trust even those within his or her own ranks. Through years of loss and mistreatment, of feeling dehumanized, disfigured, disgraced, and disenfranchised, the formerly enslaved drew together in community and learned to live with hope. "The oppressor would discover that the downtrodden cannot be destroyed forever, because God forever stands against those who exercise…mastery over the least of his children."[157] They never stopped singing, they never stopped praying, they never stopped praising, and they never stopped hoping. These contemplative acts served to solidify African-Americans in a manner that is evident even to this day.

Success will come when this generation of African-Americans:

1. Shall divorce themselves from those fragmented, naturalistic tendencies toward self-aggrandizement

2. Engage with their rich African-American heritage traditions

3. Reclaim their connection to a sovereign and loving God

My prayer is that our people will commit to a community that acts as a catalyst for the spiritual transformation of African-American life today.

SEVEN LET'S TAKE A CLOSER LOOK

Many say that the church is the sleeping giant. Yet, we know the church is the catalyst for change where true revival begins. Together, we can have the conversation and we can make a difference. What Say Ye?

1. Our Western sense of individualism seems to have driven us further apart. Would you share how important it is for you to stay connected? For us to stay connected?

2. This chapter suggests that something has been lost. What do you see is lost in our churches and communities?

3. How would you revive the sleeping giant, the church?

EIGHT

"Let's Have the Conversation"

> Blessed are those who hunger and thirst for righteousness, for they shall be satisfied.
>
> —MATTHEW 5:6, NASB

> I can do all things through Him who strengthens me.
>
> —PHILIPPIANS 4:13, NASB

> For out of the abundance of the heart the mouth speaks.
>
> —MATTHEW 12:34B, NRSV

I HAVE BRIEFLY described Spiritual Formation as a shaping of the heart because there is more to it than just the spiritual exercises; rather, our humanity is at stake. This is by no means a form of legalism. Dallas Willard, who is known for his writings on Christian Spiritual Formation, believes (and I agree) that "every human being thinks (has a thought life), feels, chooses, interacts with his or her body and its social context, and (more or less) integrates all of the foregoing as parts of one life. These are the essential factors in a human being, and nothing essential to human life falls outside of them."[158] If we look more closely, we will often find that our behavior, values, and beliefs conform to a system of moral standards that do not depend on God. This is moralism. Looming over our heads are world issues of famine, war, epidemics, and injustices. Clouding our minds are our own personal and family issues, and on top of that, the ever-present demands and enticements of media and technology. We spend our time tiptoeing through the tulips and do not get a chance to enjoy their beauty and aroma. Nonetheless, the cries of Christ remains the same—LOVE. This means to give more of ourselves. Jesus wished He could have done more. Hear His appeal: "Jerusalem, Jerusalem,... How often I wanted to gather your children together, as a hen gathers her chicks under her wings, but you were not willing!" (Matthew 23:37, NKJV).

Instead, many would prefer to turn to surveys and assessment tools like DISC, Myers-Briggs, or the Enneagram and use them as a means of self-identification or gratification. Though these tools provide useful information, let us not forget, huddled in the background underneath the skin, the core of humankind and our longing for acceptance and affirmation.

As I worked on this book, I also sensed the call of God to extend beyond my personal predefined boundaries and pursue cross-cultural relationships and partnerships with those who desire to learn and engage in deeper self-truths. After a period of study and learning, it is easy to return to the status quo with a sense of satisfaction and accomplishment, yet still be separated from the people in our communities.

Second, after all of the research I put into this book, I too found myself believing, as Dallas Willard does, that we, in the church, "measure things like attendance and giving, but we should be looking at more fundamental things like anger, contempt, honesty, and the degree to which people are under the thumb of their lusts."[159] To this list, I would include a lack of integrity, unforgiveness, retaliation, pride, and sexual sins—all of which stem from shame and guilt. With these insights in mind, here are the questions I have for the church:

1. How does the church universal support African-Americans in their quest toward wholeness as they address the marks left from slavery? How does the church help African-Americans to draw from the well of affirmation, unity, and love in spite of inequities in both our government and our society?

2. How do we script the message to open the hearts of humankind to truths that engage all people and not isolate or separate? How can the church harness this plague of wretched evil, this racism that wounds the soul, so we can model Christlikeness to the world?

3. When will we set aside tradition, culture, classism, education, and entitlement to meet on common ground as Jesus did with the Samaritan[160] woman at "Jacob's well"?

There is a need for collaboration. We must expand our exposure outside the confines of comfort, complacency, and ethnicity to begin engaging in dialogue with "people who don't look like us" or "think like us." It is this shared venue where the true self meets with its fallen nature. So, let the dialogue begin. For God has already prepared the hearts of not only our White brothers and sisters, but also people of color, to come to this table of discovery, compassion, understanding, and love. They are waiting for us. The Lord is waiting for us. However, this is a question for all people of color to answer in their respective contexts. We, as African-Americans, must do our part and be the answer to this last question:

4. How do African-Americans engage other ethnicities in an effort to learn to balance personal character traits and cultural differences to diffuse racism?

TWO EXAMPLES OF ENLIGHTENMENT AND CHANGE

Mark S. Kiselica, a multicultural psychologist, shares a personal story about a time when he was reading Derald Wing Sue's book *Counseling the Culturally Diverse: Theory and Practice* in a cross-cultural counseling class. As he read and reread the chapters, something happened within him. He shared:

> I...realized that over my entire life I had identified with oppressed peoples because my ancestors and my immediate family had encountered so many hardships throughout our history....My mother's family was from Ireland, and throughout the ages, they suffered severe poverty and political and cultural domination by the British. Their language, Gaelic, had been taken from them. They were forced to change the spelling of their last name. They left Ireland for a better life in America realizing that they would never be able to return to their homeland.... My paternal grandparents fled to the United States with the hope of providing something better for their children....My father was learning disabled and lame from a horrific leg injury for which he received inadequate medical care....For decades, he labored in factories under deplorable conditions that would eventually disable him. Yet, all he ever dreamed about was giving my brothers and sisters and me a

better life....They caused me to realize more fully that the historical experiences of other racial and ethnic groups were similar in some respects to those of my father...more tears swelled my eyes, tears of empathy, and tears of shame...ashamed of the fact that it had taken me so long to develop that level of empathetic understanding....How could I have been clueless? [161]

He also says,

[I was forced] to recognize my privileged position in our society because of my status as a so-called Anglo. It was upsetting to know that I, a member of white society, benefited from the hardships of others that were caused by a racist system. I was also disturbed by the painful realization that I was, in some ways, a racist. I had to come to grips with the fact that I had told and laughed at racist jokes and, through such behavior, had supported white racist attitudes. If I really wanted to become an effective, multicultural psychologist, extended and profound self-reckoning was in order. At times, I wanted to flee from this unpleasant process by merely participating superficially with the remaining task... while avoiding any substantive self-examination. [162]

Even though we cannot say, from this testimony alone, that Kiselica is a Christian, we can conclude that God's Spirit is at work, driving him toward truth. In Kiselica's reflection on his past, he acknowledges the support and reassurance from his colleagues during his training as a multicultural psychologist that made him feel accepted as he experienced the growing pains of his vocation. Further, when he served at a community mental health center, Kiselica recognized his "White privilege position in our society because of his status as an Anglo."[163] Kiselica's bias crushed him, but it also caused him to realize that racism hurts Whites as well as ethnic minorities. Now he understands that, in his early years, he missed opportunities to build relationships with other minorities because his segregated world discouraged intercultural contact.

For acceptance to take place, we must have a sincere coming together of minds, wills, and hearts grounded in love and truth. When the Holy Spirit is our guide and the Bible is our focal point, we can avoid the deceptive practices, indifferences, or stereotypes we've experienced in the past because of hidden systems at work in our government and society overall. Then the Eurocentric worldview of individualization will no longer nullify our efforts to gather. The heart of humankind needs to be renewed. Without this, despair sets in.

Like the enlightened Kiselica, the dominant culture and other people of color should consider becoming more inquisitive about affairs outside of their own culture. As for African-Americans overall, if we are to understand the "times,"[164] learning and embracing the historical and traditional tendencies of other cultures are invaluable and vice versa. "Caring" says that one should be prepared "to make a defense to everyone who asks you to give an account for the hope that is in you, yet with gentleness and reverence" (1 Peter 3:15b, NASB).

If the body of believers is to be prepared for the work of the kingdom, when and how will the community take seriously the call to love with empathy those unlike us?

By observing Kiselica's inward journey of ten years, one grasps a better understanding of the White struggle and its deception. See Kiselica's words:

> Yes, I was one of the good guys....But I was wrong, blinded by the insular world...a world of well-meaning whites in an era of racial segregation that dictated little contact with people who were different from me; a world that socialized American whites, including me, to be racist....I was both a product and an architect of a racist culture.... Should I continue to confront my ethnocentrism and racism and experience all of the discomfort that goes with that process or should I retreat from that process and go on living my life of comfort in my white-dominated world?...I realized I had an obligation to my ancestors to confront my fears and cultural biases, for without further growth on my part, I would continue to do to others what had been done to my ancestors....I was inspired to learn about people who were culturally different from me. I had not thought of myself as a racial being nor considered my role as a white person in a racist society....I realized that we will never make progress on racial problems that have plagued our country unless whites like me are willing to accept and manage the pain and discomfort associated with negotiating racial issues...and promote racial harmony.[165]

Kiselica made a choice and it took time. Kiselica realized he had an obligation to his ancestors to confront his fears and cultural bias. He was now on a path to learn more about the history and experiences of people of color who were culturally different. It was painful for Kiselica to address his issues; he chose not to maintain a false sense of indifference and self-deception, but to come face-to-face with his dark side. Maybe Kiselica didn't have access to the biblical tools toward wholeness—a Bible, the spiritual disciplines, or even a Christian spiritual guide or mentor as foundational to the transformation process. The point is that Kiselica was intentional.

A RIGHTEOUS STAND: DIETRICH BONHOEFFER

Now that we have heard from Kiselica, let us look at the heart and faith journey of a more prominent figure in Christendom: Dietrich Bonhoeffer, a White German theologian and scholar. He is the author of the famous *The Cost of Discipleship*. His journey was a search for divine truth that forged a lifestyle of discipleship and ultimately cost him his life.

Burdened by the rise of the Nazi regime, German nationalism, the plight of the Jews in Germany, and the fate of Christianity in his homeland, Bonhoeffer, at the age of twenty-four, accepted the Sloane Fellowship to study at Union Theological Seminary in New York City in 1930. He left Germany in a mental fog, disillusioned by seminary teaching and sermons from the pulpit. He was sure there must be more.

Yet, soon after his arrival in the States, he experienced, in this country, the familiar poverty, lack, and discrimination he had witnessed in his homeland. During his studies at Union, he found the seminary teaching and pulpit messages of the White churches still lacking in depth. He saw that they had exchanged the truth of the Gospel for a liberation theology that fostered liberal congregations operating "as a social corporation...or churches operating as charities."[166]

Bonhoeffer's search for truth continued as one Sunday he joined Albert Fisher, a Negro and Sloane Fellow awardee at Union, for a church service at Abyssinian Baptist Church in Harlem. This was in the middle of the great Harlem Renaissance. Stirred by the Negro spirituals and the purity of the messages on the Gospel of Christ, the cross, sin, forgiveness, and life and death, which were his cornerstones, Bonhoeffer made Abyssinian home base and served faithfully where needed. Bonhoeffer had found not only a home at Abyssinian but also a place of community, a place to connect with others and reconnect with his faith. He found a safe place.

In fact, that is why I think Bonhoeffer's example is one worth looking at in this chapter on having the conversation. Bonhoeffer was a man on a journey of Spiritual Formation, and in that journey, he allowed community (along with the Word of God and the spiritual disciplines) to transform his life. He mingled with members of the congregation and was welcomed into their homes for fellowship and ongoing conversation. He wanted to learn.

His enthusiasm took him to the tables of some of the most prominent Blacks in the nation—the likes of W. E. B. DuBois, Booker T. Washington, and Alain Locke. He visited one of the most prestigious schools on the East Coast: Howard University in Washington, DC, a hub for great minds and future Black political leaders. When he was not at church, stimulating conversations with the other fellows at Union continued to feed him. Here we see diversity and inclusivity working in community. These African-American Christians accepted Bonhoeffer, with his doubts and concerns laid at the cross, and enabled him to refresh his desire for intimacy with his heavenly Father. In essence, he "had to allow himself to be vulnerable by seeing himself and society from the perspective of others"[167]—a place of spiritual transformation. This "helped him to understand more clearly the dilemma of the Jews, and globally, the struggle of German nationalism against the German Christian church."[168]

When the fellowship ended at Union Theological Seminary, he returned to his beloved Germany with his soul refreshed and inspired. He embraced the nuances of the Spirit-filled life and spiritual practices within community, returning with the Negro publications and memoirs, gramophone records of Negro spirituals, and other publications that became part of his teaching tools for classes and to share with friends. A genuine life of goodwill and unity with one another arose as it flows in a life entirely dedicated to the Lord. This time destiny waited.

When Bonhoeffer returned to Germany, he was relentless in his passion to fight against the evil perpetuated by the Nazi regime. In his biography on Bonhoeffer, Eberhard Bethge writes that upon Bonhoeffer's return to Germany, "something occurred during these months that is hard for us to perceive fully, though its effects are plain. He himself would never have called it a conversion. But a change occurred in him that led to all that was to follow during this phase of his life—Discipleship."[169]

That transformation started, as we have learned, in Bonhoeffer's attendance at a Black church in America and in his labors there with his fellow believers. Bonhoeffer continued the spiritual practices of his daily morning devotions and prayer as he resumed his teaching assignment at the University of Berlin. Bonhoeffer's mission for Christ and its church erupted as he repeatedly spoke out publicly as a "witness for the church against corrupting Nazi racism." [170] The university eventually censored and banned Bonhoeffer from public speaking. Later, the Germans arrested and confined Bonhoeffer to Tegel prison as a Jewish sympathizer. A year passed as he awaited his trial, and he remained faithful to his daily devotions, prayer, and journaling. Even the strong and committed are challenged, and for Bonhoeffer loneliness set in. Nonetheless, the ties in the community were strong, and the personal, ongoing visits from family and friends in the movement provided strength for him even when feelings of depression oppressed him and suicide became an enviable option to living. In prison, his faith, his love for the Lord, and his stand for righteousness drew the attention of workers and prisoners alike. Many sought his wisdom, counsel, and encouraging words until his death in 1945 at the age of thirty-nine. Bonhoeffer faced death with personal faith and resolve. He wrote of his own journey:

> How should one become arrogant over successes or shaken by one's failures when one shares in God's suffering in the life of this world?...I know that it is only on the path that I have finally taken that I was able to learn this....May God lead us kindly through these times, but above all, may God lead us to himself. [171]

He died within weeks of the end of World War II in Germany. Yet, his works and letters were preserved and are just as relevant today as they were during his lifetime. Though I believe he went home to be with the Lord too soon, he went home full. Even the great Bonhoeffer saw the benefit of sitting down to the table with people he did not know, listening to stories previously untold, and waiting as thoughts and opinions unfolded. In the midst of building relationships and camaraderie within the community, Bonhoeffer's own Spirit had been revived for the cause of Christ.

Here is where the dialogue for reconciliation begins—at the table of love and acceptance. Here is where we all begin. Let us start with your story.

HOW TO HAVE THE CONVERSATION

We, as African-Americans, are not the only ones who must take this journey. If the goal is to put forth the kingdom agenda, the privileged and those of other cultures must take the journey with us. Mark S. Kiselica, after his training and internship, reasoned that "because my family had suffered but succeeded in overcoming these adversities, I owed something to them and my personal identity to commit myself to the lifelong challenge of ridding myself of racism and ethnocentrism so that I truly could help others facing difficulties that were similar to those of my ancestors." [172]

Finally, when we actually have the conversation, we must keep in mind the subliminal messages of microaggression. Microaggressions are putdowns by people of other cultures who may be unaware that they have engaged in racially demeaning ways toward people of color. When these microaggressions occur, they appear as fiery darts to the African-American spirit, especially when they occur in the church. Yet, they are no cause for alarm, for in a caring environment, one can discern that these pronouncements reveal the inner wounds and scars of our brothers and sisters in Christ. The mature believer weaves their identity in Christ and demonstrates the ability to tap into the power of the Holy Spirit to respond to the pain and suffering these messages leave behind. These believers are able to neutralize the effect of these messages by bringing comfort and peace to the misguided. We, then, become a welcoming conduit for change and reconciliation for those in the church and for those whom Christ draws.

Now and then, these messages can also be an opportunity to address societal deficiencies. They expose the traits of the inner heart that conceive evil and act in violation against our true self in Christ. By paying attention to them and discerning their meaning, we may find that "we are more alike, my friends, than we are unalike."[173] However, if we leave them uninterrupted and uninterpreted, we stand in jeopardy of contaminating vital relationships in family and community in the name of love.

When we talk in terms of a conversation or a meeting that beckons this dialogue, we must remember that everyone has a story and the Lord cares about our stories. Here is one possibility for what having the conversation could look like: it could be a gathering of free spirits who desire to see change "within and without" or who want to explore differences or who want to be catalysts of the faith. What emotions might you experience? What questions might one ask in preparation for this table talk? Here are some suggestions:

- Am I open to learn more about myself for my personal spiritual growth?

- Do I have a voice at the table? Do I have a voice at the table just because I am present? Is my voice welcomed?

- Do I have a listening ear? Am I willing to be a good listener?

- Can I set aside my preconceived bias, stereotypes, and attitudes for the good of all God's people and for the kingdom agenda?

- Is this a safe place?

- Can they be trusted? Can I be trusted?

I myself had just such an opportunity in late 2016. Five persons, including me, gathered for such a discussion. The organizer of the meeting provided the historical background for bringing diverse cultures together to have this discussion. He stated that we were there to discuss our engagement with race and relationship. It is amazing what can happen if we just begin with a conversation and invite the Holy Spirit to join us.

To start, our devotion for this meeting focused on John 9, the story of Jesus healing the man born blind from birth. As is the way of a Spiritual Formation group, we centered ourselves with a few moments of silence to set aside the day's work, worries, and accomplishments and to refocus inwardly on quieting our thoughts, the external voices of life, and our hearts, allowing sacred space for the work of the Spirit in us all. I acted as a facilitator for this group. The goal of this gathering was to encourage dialogue around race relations and relationships—all lives matter.

There are many approaches, but what follows is an account of how our particular meeting went. This is just an example, and I hope to encourage others to begin the dialogue, to share our stories, and to prayerfully, in a safe and trusting environment, trust that the Spirit of God will meet us at our point of need and help us find a common ground upon which to land. We are not here to criticize or pass judgment but to focus on what the Lord is inviting us to know, to do, and to become. Just as Kiselica, the multicultural psychologist, and the great Dietrich Bonhoeffer envisioned, the best gift we can give to our brothers and sisters in Christ is our presence, a listening ear, and an open heart of love and truth. We are here as the Body of Christ jointly fitted together with a vision for the work of the kingdom of God. See a synopsis of a conversation on race and relationship below.

A Synopsis of a Conversation on Race and Relationship

A Conversation on Race and Relationship

The Ground Rules Were:
- Everyone comes with a willingness to listen.
- Everyone comes with a desire to learn.
- We should respect everyone's story because it is important.
- Everyone has the space needed to finish his or her story.

Participants: The group consisted of one young adult male African-American, one adult male African-American, one senior female African-American, one young adult female White American (mixed White and African-American parents), and one senior adult male White American. The diversity of the group and their life experiences provided a broader perspective of their experience with relationships within the smaller stories. These stories are paramount to building the bridge of understanding to any perceived outcomes or issues.

Age Range: 30–70 years old

Background: All participants had completed their college education. Three of the participants had experience with or were currently with a Christian spiritual director or Christian spiritual guide. Three of the participants had an advanced degree. Two of the participants had been or were currently in therapy. All of the participants had done some research on their genealogy.

Group Theme: Value and Vulnerability.

Length of the Meeting: 1.5 hours

Group Discussion Focus: Prior to the meeting, there were two scenarios for each person to read. The first was the story of Mark S. Kiselica, and the second was the story of Miss Helen, a White senior homeowner, and Miss Helen's gardener, Joe, an African-American. (Both stories appear in this book.) The participants read the scenarios ahead of time and were prepared to discuss them as they related to the theme of value and vulnerability.

Synopsis/Discussion: A calm discussion ensued. Each story exposed a small but significant aspect of their journey with the Lord. Each participant shared a time in their life when they were able to benefit from their life experience (a time of value) and a bit about those times when they were vulnerable.

Feedback: The group appreciated the quiet time at the beginning of the gathering to center themselves and refocus. The group felt heard by others.

Next Steps: There was the sense of personal acceptance before God within the group regardless of each person's story. In general, there appeared to be less tension about continuing the dialogue in the future. Some expressed outright that they felt a freedom and willingness to continue with the next phase of the dialogue.

By centering our focus on the work of the Spirit and our practical experiences in this session, I was able to sense the door opening to a new kind of opportunity—to a progressive approach to a dialogue that would bring us together in community.

Perhaps you feel moved to foster such conversations yourself. For those of you who want to put this kind of conversation into practice, below are a few important factors to hosting such a dialogue:

- Preparing oneself by developing an internal calm to be present with another person
- Avoiding abrasive or imposing language that could be considered harsh or judgmental of our brothers or sisters in Christ
- Searching for our identity within our stories
- Reciting our stories in light of our relationship to God
- Prayerfully responding to God's invitation in our stories
- Learning to be present and sensitive when dialoguing with our brothers or sisters in their stories
- Learning to integrate/weave this newfound freedom to love into every aspect of our lives

I believe that all the nuances of these conversations connect to believing primarily in our identity in Christ as the Lover of our souls. It is this Christ, who sacrificed His life and yet is present, who will never leave us nor forsake us, and who daily extends the invitation to relationship.

As you begin hosting these conversations, you will see that, for each person on the journey, there will be a yearning for truth and an opportunity for the work of the Spirit.

Tapping into that Spirit unlocks the freedom "to be"—Selah! This spawns the desire to engage actively with both the beauty and the ugliness of evil in this life, just as Christ did.

In closing, we must see that our struggle causes us to relate even more to Christ within us, the hope of glory, and to long more for the guidance that transforms, heals, and brings unity.

In the end, we must embrace the reality that the seemingly disinherited are, in fact, the redeemed.

EIGHT LET'S TAKE A CLOSER LOOK

We have just read about the German pastor Dietrich Bonhoeffer's journey toward spiritual discovery and uncovering God's response to the Nazi threat to the church. In America, he found healthy relationships and fellow comrades that enabled him to discover deeper truths about himself, his relationship to God, and the country affairs that plagued him. Let's take a stroll down memory lane. You might want to journal this part.

1. In your relationships, what are you seeking? Or avoiding?

2. In your relationships, in what ways do you feel connected and known?

3. How have your relationships opened you to deeper truths that have been transformative? Where do you see fear?

4. If Jesus were to tell your story, what would He say?

AFTERWORD

Soulful Reflections

The harvest truly is plentiful, but the laborers are few.

—MATTHEW 9:37B, NKJV

MY STORY

AT THE BEGINNING of this book, I shared the story of Sophie, a little girl who lost her mother, but who left a trail of popcorn kernels behind her, so that her mother could find a way home to her.

Sophie's story is really my story: I was the little girl who lost her way, who longed to be heard, seen, and loved. Let me tell you a little more about my journey home.

In the 1900s, my grandmother moved to Washington, DC, to attend school. She married and had two children, one of whom was my mother. My mother grew up, got married, and I was born just after World War II. We lived in a Black neighborhood and were God-fearing people. In my early days, I remember attending Metropolitan Baptist Church. I loved to go to church because of Sunday school and Vacation Bible School. It was at church where I learned to read. I looked forward to reading the liturgy with the whole congregation while sitting beside my grandmother in the main service. In Sunday school, I read, listened to Bible stories, and learned to memorize Scripture. Today, I cannot help but wonder how much the memorization of Scriptures helped shape me as a teenager and young adult.

Then, one Sunday, came an altar call. I was about nine years old, and, in reality, I did not understand what was going on when my cousin and friend went forward. I did not understand what they were doing, but I went forward, too—and I did not know that I did not understand. In essence, from the beginning, I never had a real faith in Jesus Christ, and I did not know of a saving faith; I just wanted to be included. No one wants to be left behind. So, we received our baptism, and our families applauded. From that point on, I lived two very distinct lives: one with my school friends and one at church. This duplicity continued until I graduated from high school in 1964.

As a young adult, no one forced me to go to church; I wanted to be involved. However, after graduation, the only option open for young people like me was the Baptist Training Union (BTU), which met on Saturday afternoons. On one particular afternoon, as I waited outside, some of the older members arrived for class. They greeted me as they walked by, and I politely responded. Nevertheless, I did not want anything to do with those "old people." I was a seventeen-year-old girl who was trying to fit in, but I did not know how to relate with those who surrounded me. This was not an atypical feeling for any teenager; I now look back and see this as a defining moment. Like so many other African-Americans, I was just trying to find my place.

I never did attend that BTU meeting; I just went home, and, after a couple of Sundays, I stopped going to church altogether. In the years that followed, bad decisions and a failed marriage put me at a low point in life. I wanted a fresh start. I put my clothes in the back of my car and headed off to sunny California.

I eventually landed a job as a secretary with TRW, an aerospace company, located in Redondo Beach, California. At that time, from the outside, my life seemed to be going well—or so I thought, or so society led me to believe. On the surface, I looked like the American dream come true. I had a good job, my own car, my own home, and I had returned to school and completed my undergraduate education with a degree in computer science from California State University Dominguez Hills in 1985. Nevertheless, I was still empty, still searching for significance. I was still searching for something to fill the void within me, while also trying to fit into a system that seemed indifferent toward me.

I gravitated to the diversity issues while at TRW. I participated in group discussions and ad hoc meetings and attended workshops. I wanted to hear the stories of others in the work force—what they were experiencing on the job and in their private lives. I wanted them to know me. I was not alone. There were Whites in our group who also wanted recognition. As you will see in my later reflections, one just cannot shake some things. I was in a multicultural environment and watching employees struggle—employees of all nationalities, at all different levels of the employment spectrum, from the facilities person to the vice president. One year an employee could be on top of the pedestal of success, and the next year he or she could get a layoff notice.

In November 1989, my mother was hospitalized and later diagnosed with leukemia. The prognosis did not look good. Twice, I flew back to Washington, DC, to spend time with her. My second trip was over the Christmas holidays. By the time

I arrived, she was in the ICU and not expected to live past the first chemotherapy treatment. I could not help but see more of Sophie's popcorn kernels on the path before me. An old high school friend, Orlando, then serving in an official capacity in the Episcopal church, often came to the hospital to sit with me. It was like being visited by an angel. His presence helped to ease the grieving process and helped me recognize how much my life intertwined with the life of my mother. I was weak and nostalgic, but this too served a purpose. She held on through the holidays, but by the first week in January, my mother had gone home to be with her Lord. I was so thankful to have had that time with her, and as I look back, I realize my duplicitous life was ending.

The days after Mama's passing were hard. The community loved her, and many of her friends sent cards and gifts to encourage me. Nevertheless, this was not enough to soothe a daughter's longing. These kindnesses brought sadness as I was constantly reminded of how much I missed her. Then, as before, the Lord sent another angel to stand at my side. My good friend Darlene, a devout White Christian, called me daily to help me recover and regain my foothold on life. Again, more kernels on the path to find my way home! It worked. Though still unsaved, I was up and making progress as Darlene discipled me.

Almost a year had passed, and I was still moving slow. I had little or no inner strength. It was as though I were marching double-time in place and going nowhere. Then, I had an automobile accident. For a brief moment in time, I was not sure whether I would live or die. It is interesting what goes through one's mind in times of severe trauma. I had celebrated my mother's "homegoing," and I had no concern for my own soul. I thought I would suffer severe injury and lose everything. Things and stuff seemed to be all that mattered. *Isn't it interesting how one can be so near and yet so far from Christ!* This accident, a turning point in my life, was another trail of popcorn kernels that led me home. I cried out, "God, you've got me." I did not know what to do next, but a short time later a coworker, Adriann, came to mind.

Adriann was the only person I knew on my job who was always talking about Jesus when we would all eat lunch together. The rest of us did not take too seriously what she had to say, when in reality she was utterly trying to save our souls. Like most people, I had no idea what Adriann was saying or what Jesus was offering me. The car accident left me traumatized, and I knew that I needed to talk to her.

One day, not long after the accident, I was preparing to drive home from work when I saw Adriann in the parking lot. I flagged her down to tell her what had happened to me. As I relayed the details of my accident, she heard my inner cry for help and asked if I was ready to give my life to Christ. Not knowing what else to say, I simply replied, "Yes."

It was cold that evening, but Adriann got out of her car and came around to the driver's side of my vehicle. As for me, this lazy, wannabe saint, I rolled down the window and just sat in the comfort of a nice warm car as Adriann stood in the cold night air and offered me Christ. It did not stop there; she gave me my first Bible and took me to church. Through prayer, I landed at Faithful Central Bible Church. I was baptized there, and I have served there for over twenty-five years. As I recount this experience, I begin to tear up at the thought of how the light of love's affections was manifested in my life, and how the Lord lovingly drew me unto Himself that cold night.

Now let us shift to more recent family matters. I faithfully attended Bible study wanting to be assured that I had made the right decision, and I did. The Gospel story became alive within me. I served in ministry and in January 1996 married Fred Darby, a wonderful man who loved the Lord. After 30 years of service, I retired from TRW in 2005 to spend more time with my husband, and I longed to go to seminary. Then, my mentor called to tell me that the Lord told her to tell me to go back to school. This was another kernel of popcorn for me because it was confirmation of my next steps in life. Fred, at the age of 69, and I returned to school. In 2006, I enrolled at Talbot School of Theology at Biola University, in La Mirada, California. I was the oldest person in every class including the graduation class. That did not matter. I just wanted to learn, and I enjoyed every day that I went to school. During my time at Biola, two classes were fundamental to my development—one titled African Theology and the other titled Social Conflicts. Here I met other Africans and people of color. The discussions and interactions during class time opened my eyes because I was the misinformed and uninformed. The stories of culture and tradition moved me, and I wanted more. So in April 2010, my husband, Fred, and I hosted a social for Africans and African-Americans where we shared a little of our faith journeys. We were humbled and honored all at the same time. You see, our preconceived notions emerged, we realized we were ill informed, and our stereotypes surfaced—all in one meeting.

God was with us, and the prayers of the saints hovered over us. There were times when the words of prayer were like a vacuum—empty. That is when the spiritual disciplines I practiced at seminary filled my heart. I was able to remind myself that, for Fred and me, our identity was in Christ and we belonged to the Beloved community. The Lord continuously made melody in my soul just as He had done for the souls of my ancestors during slavery. Why should tragedy and trial be our barometers to evaluate the biblical truths on which we have come to depend? Yet, God uses those trials and tragedies to get our attention and to remind us that He is almighty and loves His people unconditionally. The Lord showed me how to love in a greater way in tough times.

It was the sense of community and the semester retreats that changed my life while at Biola. I felt cared about, known, and accepted. Yes, I was still on my guard (my trust issues surfaced), and I did at times ask the Lord, "Is this real?" My retreats were silent retreats. On the retreats, questions and issues of my personal life and past began to surface during my time with the Lord. My perceptions were altered to include a broadened view of my concept of God as a Father. In the midst of all this, healing took place, and the suppressed little girl inside reappeared. I named her Precious because she is an integral part of me, neglected for many years. Precious and I needed the Balm of Gilead, and in time, I saw changes in my inner being; I was becoming whole. Healing takes time.

In 2010, I graduated from Biola's Institute for Spiritual Formation. I was so passionate about my own life journey; I wanted to bring Spiritual Formation into the Black church and community. I told God, "If you send two, I will go," not knowing that profession would land me in Kenya in 2014, where I introduced centering prayer to the Agape Fellowship Church. I then traveled to Uganda East Africa, where I facilitated two Spiritual Formation seminars: one with Agape Global Missions and the other with a group of pastors, leaders, and psychologists. I went to Africa to learn the culture; I wanted to be relevant. They caught the vision, and for two and a half years, with the help of missionaries Dr. Linda Marcell and Rev. Manuela Glenn of Agape Global Missions, I had the privilege of teaching these timeless principles of Spiritual Formation. The Lord revealed that Uganda was fertile ground for Spiritual Formation and spiritual mentoring, teaching, and training. I am committed.

Then I found that my work at Biola was not complete. I needed more. Having the theoretical knowledge was great, but how do I practice it, what is the process, and how do I engage my brothers and sisters in the work of the Spirit that transforms lives? So, I returned to the campus to complete the Soul Care classes needed for me to become a spiritual director, after which Biola hired me as a part-time staff director to meet with students, staff, and faculty.

I loved my community of spiritual directors; however, I still longed to network with other spiritual directors of color. Membership in Spiritual Directors International (SDI) opened the door for me to meet with a small group of spiritual directors of color. After six years of informal gathering, the network was incorporated in 2014 as the Spiritual Directors of Color Network, Ltd., of which I am a member. Its members wrote two collective treatises titled *Embodied Spirits* (2014) and *Ain't Gonna Let Nobody Turn Me Around* (2017), which chronicle their journey as trailblazers in the vocation of Spiritual Formation and spiritual direction. Another treatise that centers around the spirituality of people of color, *Kaleidoscope*, was published in December 2019. Now I, and others like me, have access to other spiritual directors, supervisors, mentors, coaches, and chaplains across the globe. Praise the Lord.

TIMES ARE A-CHANGING

Repeatedly, our tabloids have bombarded us with headlines that taunt me with the shattering tragedy of a global pandemic[174], terrorism, the lost lives of both youth and adults, and attacks by and on law enforcement. These news events have also helped me to see even more noticeably that this is the *fourth watch.*[175] Just as a sense of urgency stirred within the disciples as they were trying to row to the other side of the waters, a sense of urgency stirred within me also. Because of these social pressures that affect family, the nation, and the globe, in 2015, I birthed IN HIS PRESENCE CENTER FOR SPIRITUAL TRANSFORMATION, a nonprofit organization committed to awakening and preparing the human soul for personal transformation that influences the lives of others. I am honored to head up this center, which serves as a facilitating, teaching, and training resource for concepts and principles of Spiritual Formation globally.

A TIME OF DELIVERANCE

Educational pursuits landed me, in 2015, at CenterQuest, an international organization designed to help people attend to their own ongoing personal formation and to assist in the

Spiritual Formation journey of others. It was during that training, while fulfilling an assignment of silence and solitude, that I sensed the Lord more intimately, and I began to notice negative thoughts from my past surfacing. At first, I ignored them, but the memories of racism, oppression, discrimination, and bigotry—from my own life, and from the lives of my mother and grandmother—continued. I was in a good place, just me and God, when these snapshots of repressed episodes of injustices resurfaced. I learned that, even in the high times of great intimacy with the Lord, one must still fight against those reoccurring negative thoughts that seem to find their way to the surface—those times when it may appear that the Lord is not even present. Truly, the wheat and the tares grow together. In this case, I needed to take a closer look at the past memories that seemed to haunt me. That week, my homework assignment was to write about my experience. Below is an excerpt from the assignment—more so, below is my encounter with the Holy Spirit:

> Even in these times of silence and newfound freedoms, the taunts of past experiences and attitudes continue to hover to expose bad decisions, disgraces, flaws, and failures. Remembrances of bias and racial slurs and oppressions for my family and me, and our cultural oppression, along with the history of slavery overall, became spikes in this journey. Finally, I found words for my feelings—it seems similar to the thorn about which Paul prayed. I would ask myself where and why these images are appearing, when it seems that I am reaching a new milestone in the

faith. On the other hand, have I? Marvin Gaye had it right, "Lord, what's going on?" I wonder if this is my cloud of unknowing or has freedom unleashed deeper hurts? All I wanted is love and acceptance. Is this the means by which I see what is within me? Is this as Richard Rohr, author of *Everything Belongs*, puts it, "the moments of hell come when everything militates against the open heart"[176] to taunt me? So I fight, I try to stand against the fiery darts that would sway my soul. So, this morning I took authority over this spirit of deception that would cause me to cower in the face of triumph of a greater awareness of my identity in Christ and a broadened insight into love for God; it has many faces. I put on the Lord Jesus Christ, I put on faith, love, and joy, for before time, Psalm 139 says that I am beautifully and wonderfully made, marvelous is God's handiwork and this my soul knows thus well…Now your servant is set free to go in peace. Amen.

As I continued the search inwardly, hovering behind my childhood and adult memories and the societal impacts, a remnant of caregivers emerged who befriended me, spent time with me as we walked down the road less traveled, cried with me, laughed with me—and they didn't look like me. They overlooked the chip on my shoulder, my mistrust and suspicions, and saw something of rich value. Yet, I defied their truth, for it was easier to hold on to the negative—the past. Anger overshadowed vulnerability.

There was no middle of the road for me as I saw and experienced the face of the pain of lost dreams, discrimination, alcoholism, a broken marriage, and bitterness. This becomes my story and *Everything Belongs*. The status quo becomes the one who needs healing, and the victim seems to become a castaway in their eyes. Yet, my story is not over. Those fiery darts are not as painful, because my lens has broadened. I remember a time when I would have couched my experience in vague words that hide, such as "the plight of the marginal," "uncontrollable circumstances," "silent killer," or "a dismal time in history." Not today, for underneath the lies of the false self is another layer of inner clues to wrestle with: remnants of slavery and its impact on my adult life.

Finally, it is priority and perspective. When my greatest joy is to release fear and trust that the Lord is at work for my good, when my heart's desire is to seek Him (Matthew 6:33-34) and to want to know Him more (John 17:3), and when I can look past my faults and see the need, the sting of pain reduces. Slowing down and/or calming down becomes a way to experience visual glimpses of God's creation; pictures, music, sunrises, and sunsets are reminders of the Beauty of the Lord. Studying and sharing with others of like minds helped. All is designed to develop a divine contemplative seeing that will feed and fill the voids left by my pain and suffering and bring about a fresh awareness of love's call.

My experience at the CenterQuest program reinforced within me the importance of spiritual restoration among all people groups. In humility, they heard my story and I heard theirs. We got to know each other. We laughed together, ate together, roomed together, and prayed together. It was safe and sacred, and my spirit was reawakened to the importance of becoming sensitive to the diversity of our cultures, our value systems, and our areas of vulnerability—things that can (and often do) separate us. How then do we move from diversity to a sense of feeling connected or to inclusivity? We must keep at the forefront of our minds that we are all a part of God's creation. With that being said, a melody blossoms in my spirit. It is the lyrics from "I Need You to Survive," a song sung by Hezekiah Walker:

> *I need you, you need me.*
> *We're all a part of God's body.*
> *Stand with me, agree with me.*
> *We're all a part of God's body.*
>
> *It is his will, that every need be supplied.*
> *You are important to me, I need you to survive.*
> *You are important to me, I need you to survive.*
> *I pray for you, you pray for me.*
>
> *I love you, I need you to survive.*
> *I won't harm you with words from my mouth.*
> *I love you, I need you to survive.*[177]

After God created humankind, "God saw everything that he had made, and indeed, it was very good" (Genesis 1:31a, NRSV). I cannot improve on perfection, but with God's help, I can improve on me and face my demons. Now, I can sing.

APPENDIX
Black Inventors and Inventions

Invention	Inventor	Date
Air Conditioning Unit	Frederick M. Jones	July 12, 1949
Almanac	Benjamin Banneker	Approx. 1791
Auto Cut-Off Switch	Granville T. Woods	January 1, 1839
Auto Fishing Devise	G. Cook	May 30, 1899
Automatic Gear Shift	Richard Spikes	February 28, 1932
Baby Buggy	W. H. Richardson	June 18, 1899
Bicycle Frame	L.R. Johnson	October 10, 1899
Biscuit Cutter	A.P. Ashbourne	November 30, 1875
Blood Plasma Bag	Charles Drew	Approx. 1945
Cellular Phone	Henry T. Sampson	July 6, 1971
Chamber Commode	T. Elkins	January 3, 1897
Clothes Dryer	G.T. Sampson	June 6, 1862
Curtain Rod	S.R. Scratton	November 30, 1889
Curtain Rod	William S. Grant	August 4, 1896
Door Stop	O. Dorsey	December 10, 1878
Dust Pan	Lawrence P. Ray	August 3, 1897
Egg Beater	Willie Johnson	February 5, 1884
Electric Lampbulb	Lewis Latimer	March 21, 1882
Elevator	Alexander Miles	October 11, 1867
Eye Protector	P. Johnson	November 2, 1880
Fire Escape Ladder	J.W. Winters	May 7, 1878
Folding Bed	L.C. Bailey	July 18, 1899
Folding Chair	Brody & Surgwar	June 11, 1889
Fountain Pen	W.B. Purvis	January 7, 1890
Furniture Caster	O.A. Fisher	1878
Gas Mask	Garrett Morgan	October 13, 1914
Golf Tee	T. Grant	December 12, 1899
Guitar	Robert F. Flemming, Jr.	March 3, 1886
Hair Brush	Lydia O. Newman	November 15, 18--

Invention	Inventor	Date
Hand Stamp	Walter B. Purvis	February 27, 1883
Horse Shoe	J. Ricks	March 30, 1885
Ice Cream	A.L. Cralle	February 2, 1897
Insect-Destroyer Gun	A.C. Richard	February 28, 1899
Ironing Board	Sarah Boone	December 30, 1887
Key Chain	F.J. Loudin	January 9, 1894
Lantern	Michael c. Harvey	August 19, 1884
Lawn Mower	L.A. Burr	May 19, 1889
Lemon Squeezer	J. Thomas White	December 8, 1893
Lock	W.A. Martin	July 23, 18--
Lubricating Cup	Ellijah McCoy	November 15, 1895
Lunch Pail	James Robinson	1887
Mail Box	Paul L. Downing	October 27, 1891
Mop	Thomas W. Stewart	June 11, 1893
Motor	Frederick M. Jones	June 27, 1939
Peanut Butter	George Washington Carver	1896
Pencil Sharpener	J.L. Love	November 23, 1897
Phone Transmitter	Granville T. Woods	December 2, 1884
Record Player Arm	Joseph Hunger Dickenson	January 8, 1819
Refrigerator	J. Standard	June 14, 1891
Riding Saddles	W.D., Davis	October 6, 1895
Rolling Pin	John W. Reed	1864
Shampoo Headrest	C.O. Bailiff	October 11, 1898
Spark Plu	Edmond Berger	February 2, 1839
Stethoscope	Imhotep	Ancient Egypt
Stove	T.A. Carrington	July 25, 1876
Straightening Comb	Madam C.J. Walker	Approx. 1905
Street Sweeper	Charles B. Brooks	March 17, 1890
Sugar Making	Norbet Rillieux	December 10, 1846
Thermostat Control	Frederick M. Jones	February 23, 1960
Traffic Light	Garrett Morgan	November 20, 1923
Tricycle	M.A. Cherry	May 6, 1886
Typewriter	Burridge & Marshman	April 7, 1885

BIBLIOGRAPHY

Akbar, Na'im. *Breaking the Chains of Psychological Slavery*. Tallahassee, FL: Mind Productions and Associates, 1997.

Albert, Octavia V. Rogers. *The House of Bondage, or, Charlotte Brooks and Other Slaves*. New York: Hunt & Eaton, 1891.

Anderson, Louis P., Chuck L. Eaddy, and Ernestine A. Williams. "Psychosocial Competence: Toward a Theory of Understanding Positive Mental Health among Black Americans." In *Handbook of Mental Health and Mental Disorder among Black People*, edited by Dorothy S. Ruiz, 255-72. Westport, CT: Greenwood Press, 1990.

Anderson, Terry. *The Pursuit of Fairness: A History of Affirmative Action*. Oxford, UK: Oxford University Press, 2004.

Angelou, Maya. *The Complete Poetry*. New York: Random House, 2015.

Anyabwile, Thabiti M. *The Decline of African American Theology: From Biblical Faith to Cultural Captivity*. Downers Grove, IL: IVP Academic, 2007.

Awosan, Christina I., Jonathan G. Sandberg, and Cadmona A. Hall. "Understanding the Experience of Black Clients in Marriage and Family Therapy." *Journal of Marital and Family Therapy* 37, no. 2 (April 2011): 153–68.

Axelrod, Alan. *Minority Rights in America*. Washington, DC: CQ Press, 2002.

Balswick, Jack O., Pamela Ebstyne King, and Kevin S. Reimer. *The Reciprocating Self*. Downers Grove, IL: IVP Academic, 2005.

Beasley-Topliffe, Keith ed. *The Upper Room Dictionary of Christian Spiritual Formation*. Nashville, TN: Upper Room Books, 2003.

Benner, David G. *Care of Souls; Revisioning Christian Nurture and Counsel*. Grand Rapids, MI: Baker Books, 1998.

Bethge, Eberhard. *Dietrich Bonhoeffer: A Biography*. Minneapolis: Fortress Press, 2000.

Bonhoeffer, Dietrich. *Letters and Papers from Prison—Reader's Edition*. English. Edited by John W. de Gruchy. Minneapolis: Fortress Press, 2015.

Boyd-Franklin, Nancy. *Black Families in Therapy: A Multisystems Approach*. New York: The Guilford Press, 1989.

_____. *Black Families in Therapy: Understanding the African American Experience*, 2nd ed. New York: The Guilford Press, 2006.

Bryant-Johnson, Sherry, Rosalie Norman-McNaney, and Therese Taylor-Stinson. *Embodied Spirits: Stories of Spiritual Directors of Color*. Harrisburg, PA: Morehouse Publishing, 2014.

Burrell, Tom. *Brainwashed: Challenging the Myth of Black Inferiority*. New York: Smiley Books, 2010.

Comer, James P., and Alvin F. Poussaint. *Black Child Care*. New York: Pocket Books, 1979.

Cone, James H. *The Spirituals and the Blues*. Maryknoll, NY: Orbis Books, 1991.

Cooper-Lewter, Nicholas, and Henry H. Mitchell. *Soul Theology: The Heart of American Black Culture*. Nashville, TN: Abingdon Press, 1991.

DeGruy-Leary, Joy. "Post Traumatic Slave Syndrome with Dr. Joy DeGruy-Leary." https://overtroubledwater.blogspot.com/2011/07/post-traumatic-slave-syndrome-with-dr.html.

Evangelical Dictionary of Theology, 2nd ed. Grand Rapids, MI: Baker Academic, 2001.

"Fugitive Slave Case: Stephen Pembrook," National Archives, https://www.archives.gov/nyc/exhibit/stephen-pembrook.html.

Grier, William H., and Price M. Cobbs. *Black Rage*. New York: BasicBooks, 1980.

Griffin, Paul R. "Protestantism and Racism." *In The Blackwell Companion to Protestantism*, edited by Alister E. McGrath and Darren C. Marks, 357–71. Malden, MA: Blackwell Publishing, 2004.

Herskovits, Melville J. *The Myth of the Negro Past*. Boston: Beacon Press, 1958.

Kelleman, Robert W., and Karole A. Edwards. *Beyond the Suffering: Embracing the Legacy of African American Soul Care and Spiritual Direction*. Grand Rapids, MI: Baker Books, 2007.

Kiselica, Mark S. "Preparing Anglos for the Challenges and Joys of Multiculturalism." *The Counseling Psychologist* 26: no. 1 (January 1, 1998): 5–21.

Krause, Lisa. "Black Soldiers in WWII: Fighting Enemies at Home and Abroad." *National Geographic News*, February 15, 2001.

Lewter, Nicholas Cooper, and Henry H. Mitchell. *Soul Theology: The Heart of American Black Culture*. Nashville, TN: Abingdon Press, 1986.

Locke, Alain, ed. *The New Negro: Voices of the Harlem Renaissance*. New York: Touchstone, 1925.

Lynch, W. *The Slave Consultants Narrative*. Source unknown: 1712.

Mbiti, John S. *African Religions and Philosophy*. Garden City, NY: Doubleday, 1969.

_____. *African Religions and Philosophy*, 2nd ed., rev. ed. Garden City, NY: Doubleday, 1990.

_____. *Introduction to African Religion*. New York: Praeger Publishers, 1975.

_____ *Introduction to African Religion*, 2nd ed. Long Grove, IL: Waveland Press, 2015.

Merriam-Webster Collegiate Dictionary, 11th ed. Springfield, MA: Merriam-Webster, 2003. Continually updated at https://www.merriam-webster.com/.

Mitchell, Henry H. *Black Belief: Folk Beliefs of Blacks in America and West Africa*. San Francisco: Harper & Row, 1975.

_____. *Black Church Beginnings: The Long-Hidden Realities of the First Years*. Grand Rapids, MI: Eerdmans, 2004.

Mulholland, M. Robert, Jr. *Invitation to a Journey*. Downers Grove, IL: IVP Books, 1993.

The New Encyclopaedia Britannica. 15th ed. 32 vols. Chicago: Encyclopaedia Britannica, 2010. Final print version. Continued online, as Encyclopaedia Britannica, at https://www.britannica.com/.

Noll, Mark A. *A History of Christianity in the United States and Canada*. Grand Rapids, Ml: Eerdmans, 1992.

Potok, Mark. "The Year in Hate and Extremism." *Intelligence Report*. February 15, 2017. http://www.library.georgetown.edu/tutorials/research-guides/turabian-footnote-guide#magonline.

Quiller-Couch, Arthur Thomas, ed. *The Oxford Book of English Verse*, 1250-1900, 1st (6th impression) ed. Oxford, UK: Clarendon Press, 1888.

Raboteau, Albert J. *Slave Religion: The "Invisible Institution" in the Antebellum South*. New York: Oxford University Press, 2004.

Random House Dictionary of the English Language. New York: Random House, 1973.

Rodriguez, Junius P., ed. *The Historical Encyclopedia of World Slavery* vol. 2 L-Z. Santa Barbara, CA: ABC-CLIO, 1997.

Rohr, Richard. *Everything Belongs: The Gift of Contemplative Prayer*. New York: The Crossroad Publishing Company, 2003.

Ruiz, Dorothy S. "Social and Economic Profile of Black Americans, 1989." In *Handbook of Mental Health and Mental Disorder among Black People*, edited by Dorothy S. Ruiz, 3–16. Westport, CT: Greenwood Press, 1990.

Ruiz, Dorothy S, ed. *Handbook of Mental Health and Mental Disorder Among Black People*. Westport, CT: Greenwood Press, 1990.

Shade, Barbara J. "Coping with Color: The Anatomy of Positive Mental Health." In *Handbook of Mental Health and Mental Disorder among Black People*, edited by Dorothy S. Ruiz, 273–90. Westport, CT: Greenwood Press, 1990.

Sue, Derald Wing, and David Sue. *Counseling the Culturally Diverse: Theory and Practice*, 5th ed. Hoboken, NJ: Wiley & Sons, 2007.

_____. *Counseling the Culturally Diverse: Theory and Practice*, 7th ed. Hoboken, NJ: Wiley & Sons, 2016.

Sue, Derald Wing. *Microaggressions in Everyday Life: Race, Gender, and Sexual Orientation*. Hoboken, NJ: Wiley & Sons, 2010.

_____. *Race Talk and the Conspiracy of Silence: Understanding and Facilitating Difficult Dialogues on Race*. Hoboken, NJ: Wiley & Sons, 2015.

Thurman, Howard. *Jesus and the Disinherited*. Boston: Beacon, 1996.

_____. *The Negro Spiritual Speaks of Life and Death*. New York: Harper and Row, 1947.

Wallace, Mike. Interview with Dr. Martin Luther King, Jr. *60 Minutes*. CBS. June 25, 1958.

Willard, Dallas. "How Do We Assess Spiritual Growth?" *Leadership Journal* 31, no. 2 (May 2010).

Willard, Dallas. *Renovation of the Heart*. Colorado Springs, CO: NavPress, 2002.

Williams, Reggie L. *Bonhoeffer's Black Jesus: Harlem Renaissance Theology and an Ethic of Resistance*. Waco, TX: Baylor University Press, 2014.

Wilmore, Gayraud S. *Black Religion and Black Radicalism: An Interpretation of the Religious History of African Americans*. Maryknoll, NY: Orbis Books, 1998.

_____. *Pragmatic Spirituality: The Christian Faith Through an Africentric Lens*. New York: New York University Press, 2004.

The Word in Life Study Bible, New Testament Edition. Nashville, TN: Thomas Nelson, 1996.

NOTES

PREFACE

[1] "Spheres" here refers to the different pillars of society, namely the Home, Religion, Politics, Business and Finance, Education, Media and the Arts. Each of these spheres has played a part in the ability of the African-American people to integrate into the American culture as a whole.

[2] Walter A Elwell, ed., *Evangelical Dictionary of Theology*, 2nd ed. (Grand Rapids, MI: Baker Academic, 2001), s.v. "racism."

[3] Romans 8:2: "And because you belong to him, the power of the life-giving Spirit has freed you from the power of sin that leads to death" (NLT).

ONE

[4] A cultural conditioning factor occurs when events in our lives start to shape our character, behavior, and response to societal issues.

[5] While the exact composition of this list of four cultural conditioning factors is my own, I developed this list in conversation with the work of other scholars. I am particularly indebted to the work of Dr. Alexis Abernethy, Dr. Derald Wing Sue, Dr. Albert Raboteau, Dr. Nancy Boyd-Franklin, and Dr. Henry Mitchell.

[6] David G. Benner, *Care of Souls: Revisioning Christian Nurture and Counsel* (Grand Rapids, MI: Baker Books, 1998), 78.

[7] M. Robert Mulholland, Jr., *Invitation to a Journey* (Downers Grove, IL: IVP Books, 1993), 47.

[8] Benner, 23.

[9] Ibid., 21.

TWO

[10] John Mbiti, *African Religions and Philosophy* (Garden City, NY: Doubleday, 1969), 19.

11 John Mbiti, *African Religions and Philosophy*, 2nd ed., rev. ed. (Garden City, NY: Doubleday, 1990), 19.

12 Jack O. Balswick, Pamela Ebstyne King, and Kevin S. Reimer, *The Reciprocating Self* (Downers Grove, IL: IVP Academic, 2005), 266.

13 John Mbiti, *Introduction to African Religion*, 2nd ed. (Long Grove, IL: Waveland Press, 2015), 45–46.

14 Henry H. Mitchell, *Black Belief: Folk Beliefs of Blacks in America and West Africa* (San Francisco: Harper & Row, 1975), 69.

15 Ibid., 70.

16 Benner, 52.

17 Mbiti, *Introduction to African Religion*, 2nd ed., 179.

18 Ibid., 2.

19 Mbiti, *African Religions and Philosophy*, 2nd ed., rev. ed., 4.

20 Ibid., 6.

21 Ibid., 20.

22 John Mbiti, *Introduction to African Religion* (New York: Praeger Publishers, 1975), 57.

23 Ibid., 57, 59.

24 *Random House Dictionary of the English Language* (New York: Random House, 1973). s.v. "slavery."

25 Junius P. Rodriguez, ed., *The Historical Encyclopedia of World Slavery*, vol. 2, L-Z (Santa Barbara, CA: ABC-CLIO, 1997), 469.

26 The Door of No Return is an exhibit at the historical museum House of Slaves. This door was the last thing our ancestors saw of the motherland before boarding slave ships to the Americas.

27 Benner, 101.

THREE

[28] Hugh Thomas, *The Slave Trade* (New York: Touchstone, 1990), 804.

[29] Paul R. Griffin, "Protestantism and Racism," ed. Alister E. McGrath and Darren C. Marks, *The Blackwell Companion to Protestantism* (Malden, MA: Blackwell Publishing, 2004), 362.

[30] Thabiti M. Anyabwile, *The Decline of African American Theology: From Biblical Faith to Cultural Captivity* (Downers Grove, IL: IVP Academic, 2007), 68.

[31] Gayraud S. Wilmore, *Black Religion and Black Radicalism: An Interpretatiaon of the Religious History of African Americans* (Maryknoll, NY: Orbis Books, 1998), 69.

[32] Na'im Akbar, *Breaking the Chains of Psychological Slavery* (Tallahassee, FL: Mind Productions and Associates, 1997), 30–31.

[33] Ibid., 31.

[34] See, for example, the State Statue of North Carolina in 1830–1831, which prevented all persons from teaching slaves to read or write, the use of figures excepted. This was passed by the General Assembly of the State of North Carolina in the Session of 1830–1831.

[35] Willie Lynch, The Willie Lynch Letter: *The Making of a Slave!* (https://archive.org/stream/WillieLynchLetter1712/the_willie_lynch_letter_the_making_of_a_slave_1712_djvu.txt).

[36] Mitchell, Black Belief, 104.

[37] Howard Thurman, *The Negro Spiritual Speaks of Life and Death* (New York: Harper and Row, 1947), 12.

[38] Mitchell, Black Belief, 104.

[39] The Hebrew names were originally Hananiah ("Jehovah is gracious"), Mishael ("who is what God is?"), and Azariah ("Jehovah has helped"), respectively.

[40] Albert J. Raboteau, *Slave Religion: The "Invisible Institution" in the Antebellum South* (New York: Oxford University Press, 2004), 8.

41 Ibid., 103.

42 James H. Cone, *The Spirituals and the Blues* (Maryknoll, NY: Orbis Books, 1991), 57.

43 Ibid., 13.

44 Ibid., 16.

45 Author Unknown, lyrics to "Nobody Knows de Trouble I See!" https://www .negrospirituals.com/songs/i_ve_been_buked_and_ive_been_scorned.htm.

46 Author Unknown, lyrics to "Swing Low, Sweet Chariot (First Version)," https://www.negrospirituals.com/songs/ swing_low_sweet_chariot_swing_lo.htm.

47 Nicholas Cooper-Lewter and Henry H. Mitchell, *Soul Theology: The Heart of American Black Culture* (Nashville, TN: Abingdon Press, 1991), 33.

48 Cone, 59.

49 Ibid., 59.

50 J. W. Johnson and J. R. Johnson, lyrics to "Sometimes I Feel Like a Motherless Chile," 1926, https://www.negrospirituals.com/songs/ sometimes_i_fell.htm.

51 Author Unknown, lyrics to "All God's Chillun Got Wings," https://www .negrospirituals.com/songs/all_god_s_chillun_got_wings.htm.

52 Ibid.

53 Ibid.

54 J. W. Johnson and J. R. Johnson, lyrics to "Steal Away to Jesus," https://www .negrospirituals.com/songs/steal_away_to_jesus.htm.

55 Kellemen and Edwards, 157.

56 Author Unknown, lyrics to "Soon-a Will Be Done," https://www .negrospirituals.com/songs/soon_a_will_be_done.htm.

57 Ibid.

58 Ibid.

59 Author Unknown, lyrics to "I've Been 'Buked And I've Been Scorned," https://www.negrospirituals.com/songs/i_ve_been_buked_and_i-ve_been _scorned.htm.

60 Octavia V. Rogers Albert, *The House of Bondage, or, Charlotte Brooks and Other Slaves* (New York: Hunt & Eaton, 1891), 15.

61 Wilmore, *Black Religion and Black Radicalism*, 134.

62 Griffin, 362.

63 Tom Burrell, *Brainwashed: Challenging the Myth of Black Inferiority* (New York: Smiley Books, 2010), 185.

FOUR

64 The Freedmen's Bureau was established in 1865 to assist the Black former slaves and the poor Whites with food, housing, and medical aid. It established schools and offered legal assistance. A shortage of funds and personnel, along with Southern politics on race, prevented the bureau from being more effective.

65 This act mandated that "all persons born in the United States," with the exception of American Indians, "were hereby declared to be citizens of the United States." It granted all citizens the "full and equal benefit of all laws and proceedings for the security of person and property."

66 Henry H. Mitchell, *Black Church Beginnings: The Long-Hidden Realities of the First Years* (Grand Rapids, MI: Eerdmans, 2004), 52.

67 Ibid., 51–52.

68 Ibid., 48–49.

69 Raboteau, 204.

70 Ibid., 207.

71 Ibid., 213.

72 Ibid., 181.

73 Ibid., 182.

[74] Ibid., 183.

[75] Mark A. Noll, *A History of Christianity in the United States and Canada* (Grand Rapids, MI: Eerdmans, 1992), 86.

[76] Mitchell, *Black Church Beginnings*, 98.

[77] Alain Locke, ed., *The New Negro: Voices of the Harlem Renaissance* (New York: Touchstone, 1925), 6.

[78] Ibid., 6.

[79] Ibid., 7.

[80] Ibid., 7.

[81] James Weldon Johnson, "Lift Every Voice and Sing," 1900, public domain, https://www.negrospirituals.com/songs/lift_every_voice_and_sing.htm.

[82] In 1908, two reports of a Black man assaulting a White woman erupted into a White race riot in Springfield, Illinois, the home of President Abraham Lincoln. The mob rampaged the city, destroying Black homes and businesses. This was the first riot of its time in the North in over a half century and could be called the impetus to the creation of the National Association for the Advancement of Colored People (NAACP). Founded in 1909, it started as an interracial civil rights organization of educators and activists whose vision was to secure for all people the rights guaranteed by the Thirteenth, Fourteenth, and Fifteenth Amendments. The founding members were W. E. B. DuBois, Henry Moskowitz, Mary White Ovington, Oswald Garrison Villard, William English Walling, and Ida B. Wells.

[83] Lisa Krause, "Black Soldiers in WWII: Fighting Enemies at Home and Abroad," *National Geographic* News, February 15, 2001 (accessed February 27, 2017).

[84] Terry H. Anderson, *The Pursuit of Fairness: A History of Affirmative Action* (Oxford, UK: Oxford University Press, 2004), 85.

[85] Mike Wallace, Interview with Dr. Martin Luther King, Jr., *60 Minutes*, CBS, June 25, 1958.

[86] Encyclopedia Britannica, "Southern Baptist Convention," https://www.britannica.com/topic/Southern-Baptist-Convention/.

87 Mark Potok, "The Year in Hate and Extremism," *Intelligence Report*, Spring Issue, February 15, 2017, https://www.splcenter.org/fighting-hate/intelligence-report/2017/year-hate-and-extremism/.

88 Ibid.

89 Ibid.

FIVE

90 Derald Wing Sue, *Race Talk and the Conspiracy of Silence: Understanding and Facilitating Difficult Dialogues on Race* (Hoboken, NJ: Wiley & Sons, 2015), 215–16.

91 Joy DeGruy-Leary, "Post Traumatic Slave Syndrome with Dr. Joy DeGruy-Leary," Mhttps://overtroubledwater.blogspot.com/2011/07/post-traumatic-slave-syndrome-with-dr.html.

92 Sue, *Race Talk*, 107.

93 Barbara J. Shade, "Coping with Color: The Anatomy of Positive Mental Health," *Handbook of Mental Health and Mental Disorder Among Black Americans*, Dorothy S. Ruiz, ed. (Westport, CT: Greenwood Press, 1990), 277.

94 Melville J. Herskovits, *The Myth of the Negro Past* (Boston: Beacon Press, 1958), 154–55.

95 Dorothy S. Ruiz, "Social and Economic Profile of Black Americans, 1989," in Ruiz, *Handbook of Mental Health*, 3.

96 Louis P. Anderson, Chuck L. Eaddy, and Ernestine A. Williams, "Psychosocial Competence: Toward a Theory of Understanding Positive Mental Health among Black Americans," in Ruiz, *Handbook of Mental Health*, 266.

97 The author attended a meeting in November 1998, celebrating veterans at TRW, with a speaker's panel that consisted of the sons and daughters of veterans. None were able to address the son's question of why.

98 Nancy Boyd-Franklin, *Black Families in Therapy: A Multisystems Approach* (New York: The Guilford Press, 1989), 20.

[99] Boyd-Franklin, 17.

[100] Gayraud S. Wilmore, *Pragmatic Spirituality: The Christian Faith Through an Africentric Lens* (New York: New York University Press, 2004), 143.

[101] Ruiz, *Handbook of Mental Health*, 5.

[102] James P. Comer and Alvin F. Poussaint, *Black Child Care* (New York: Pocket Books, 1979), 11.

[103] Nancy Boyd-Franklin, *Black Families in Therapy: Understanding the African American Experience*, 2nd ed. (New York: The Guilford Press, 2006), 27.

[104] It was Alpha Phi Alpha that sparked the campaign for the Martin Luther King, Jr. National Memorial.

[105] Arthur Quiller-Couch, ed., *The Oxford Book of English Verse*, 1250-1900, 1st (6th impression) ed. (Oxford, UK: Clarendon Press, 1888), 1019.

SIX

[106] Boyd-Franklin, *Black Families in Therapy: Understanding the African American Experience*, 22.

[107] Ibid., 22.

[108] William H. Grier and Price M. Cobbs, *Black Rage* (New York: Basic-Books, 1980), 67.

[109] "Allan Bakke, a White man, contended that he was the victim of reverse discrimination because he was twice denied admission into a medical school that reserved sixteen slots for African-American, Latino, Asian, and Native American applicants who, under a special admissions program, were admitted with lower test scores and grade point averages than other applicants. He filed suit on the grounds that the university's special program violated Title VI of the Civil Rights Act of 1964, which barred racial or ethnic preferences in programs supported by federal funds. The higher court held that the special admissions program did, indeed, violate the equal protection clause of the Fourteenth Amendment, yet the ruling

affirmed the right of universities to take race into account as a factor in admissions." —Alan Axelrod, *Minority Rights in America* (Washington, DC: CQ Press, 2002), 235.

110 The Southern Poverty Law Center states that the extremist group White Lives Matter (a racist response to the Black Lives Matter movement) is a neo-Nazi group that is growing into a movement as more and more White supremacist groups take up its slogans and tactics.

111 "All Lives Matter" is a slogan used as a criticism of the Black Lives Matter movement. See article posted at https://www.huffingtonpost.com/john -halstead/dear-fellow-white-people-_b_11109842.html.

112 *Merriam-Webster Collegiate Dictionary*, 11th ed. (Springfield, MA: Merri-am-Webster, 2003), s.v. "mistrust," www.merriam-webster.com (accessed January 20, 2019).

113 Sue, Race Talk, 107–08.

114 Ibid., 108.

115 Ibid., 109.

116 Nancy Boyd-Franklin, *Black Families in Therapy: Understanding the African American Experience*, 23.

117 Christina I. Awosan, Jonathan G. Sandberg, Cadmona A. Hall, "Understanding the Experience of Black Clients in Marriage and Family Therapy," *Journal of Marital and Family Therapy* 37, no. 2 (April 2011): 153.

118 Boyd-Franklin, *Black Families in Therapy: A Multisystems Approach*, 105.

119 Derald Wing Sue and David Sue, *Counseling the Culturally Diverse: Theory and Practice*, 7th ed. (Hoboken, NJ: Wiley & Sons, 2016), 373.

120 Derald Wing Sue, *Microaggressions in Everyday Life: Race, Gender, and Sexual Orientation* (Hoboken, NJ: Wiley & Sons, 2010), 147.

121 Ibid., 147.

122 Sue, *Counseling the Culturally Diverse*, 7th ed., 183.

123 Sue, *Microaggressions in Everyday Life*, 28.

124 Ibid., 31.

125 Ibid., 25.

126 Ibid., 125.

127 Sue, *Race Talk*, 155.

128 Sue, *Microaggressions in Everyday Life*, 32–33.

129 The Bureau of Labor Statistics, U.S. Department of Labor, on December 7, 2018, released statistics saying that the unemployment rate for Whites was 3.1%, for Asians 2.7%, for Hispanics or Latinos 4.4%, and for Blacks or African-Americans 5.8%.

130 Note: People whose ethnicity is identified as Hispanic or Latino may be of any race. Data for Asians are only since 2000. Source: U.S. Bureau of Labor Statistics, Current Population Survey (CPS).

131 Boyd-Franklin, *Black Families in Therapy: A Multisystem Approach*, 11.

132 Sue, *Microaggressions in Everyday Life*, 145.

133 Ibid., 145.

134 Boyd-Franklin, *Black Families in Therapy: Understanding the African American Experience*, 27.

135 The five stages of the Cross model include pre-encounter, encounter, immersion-emersion, internalization, and internalization-commitment.

136 Sue, *Counseling the Culturally Diverse*, 7th ed., 360.

137 Boyd-Franklin, *Black Families in Therapy: Understanding the African American Experience*, 27.

138 Ibid., 151.

139 Ibid., 150.

140 Howard Thurman, *Jesus and the Disinherited*, (Boston: Beacon Press, 1996), 20.

SEVEN

141 "Fugitive Slave Case: Stephen Pembrook," National Archives, https://www.archives.gov/nyc/exhibit/stephen-pembrook.html.

142 Matthew 28:18-20: "And Jesus came up and spoke to them, saying, 'All authority has been given to Me in heaven and on earth. Go therefore and make disciples of all the nations, baptizing them in the name of the Father and the Son and the Holy Spirit, teaching them to observe all that I commanded you; and lo, I am with you always, even to the end of the age'" (NASB).

143 Mulholland, 47.

144 Benner, 103.

145 Ibid., 195–96.

146 Albert A. Goodson, "We've Come This Far by Faith," copyright Manna Music, 1965.

147 Wilmore, *Pragmatic Spirituality*, 95.

148 Thurman, *The Negro Spiritual*, 50.

149 Sherry Bryant-Johnson, Rosalie Norman-McNaney, and Therese Taylor-Stinson, *Embodied Spirits: Stories of Spiritual Directors of Color* (Harrisburg, PA: Morehouse Publishing, 2014), 15.

150 Thurman, *The Negro Spiritual*, 50.

151 Ibid., 49.

152 *Merriam-Webster Collegiate Dictionary*, s.v. "Afrocentricity."

153 Thurman, *The Negro Spiritual*, 53.

154 Keith Beasley-Topliffe, ed., *The Upper Room Dictionary of Christian Spiritual Formation* (Nashville, TN: Upper Room Books, 2003), 81.

155 Benner, 105.

156 Bryant-Johnson et al., 149.

157 Wilmore, *Black Religion and Black Radicalism*, 134.

EIGHT

158 Dallas Willard, *Renovation of the Heart* (Colorado Springs, CO: NavPress, 2002), 31.

159 Dallas Willard, "How Do We Assess Spiritual Growth?" *Leadership Journal* 31, no. 2 (May 2010): 22.

160 "There are countless modern parallels to the Jewish-Samaritan enmity—indeed, wherever peoples are divided by racial and ethnic barriers....It is not the person from the radically different culture on the other side of the world that is hardest to love, but the nearby neighbor whose skin color, language, rituals, values, ancestry, history, and customs are different from one's own. Jews had no dealings with the Samaritans." —The Word in Life Study Bible, New Testament Edition (Nashville, TN: Thomas Nelson, 1996), 1867.

161 Derald Wing Sue and David Sue, *Counseling the Culturally Diverse: Theory and Practice*, 5th ed., 8–9.

162 Mark S. Kiselica, "Preparing Anglos for the Challenges and Joys of Multiculturalism," The Counseling Psychologist, 26, no. 1 (January 1998): 10–11.

163 Ibid., 10.

164 See 1 Chronicles 12:32a: "Of the sons of Issachar, men who understood the times, with knowledge of what Israel should do" (NASB).

165 Sue, *Counseling the Culturally Diverse*, 7th ed., 10–13.

166 Reggie L. Williams, *Bonhoeffer's Black Jesus: Harlem Renaissance Theology and an Ethic of Resistance* (Waco, TX: Baylor University Press, 2014), 18.

167 Ibid., 79.

168 Ibid., 79.

169 Eberhard Bethge, *Dietrich Bonhoeffer: A Biography* (Minneapolis: Fortress Press, 2000), 174.

170 Ibid., 138.

[171] Dietrich Bonhoeffer, *Letters and Papers from Prison—Reader's Edition*, ed. John W. de Gruchy (Minneapolis: Fortress Press, 2015), 472.

[172] Kiselica, 11.

[173] Maya Angelou, "Human Family," *The Complete Poetry* (New York: Random House, 2015), 219.

AFTERWORD

[174] Covid-19 pandemic in 2020.

[175] The fourth watch is mentioned in Matthew 14:22-34. During Roman rule, the night was divided into four watches, which were each three hours in duration. After a day of ministry, Jesus sent His disciples across the nearby sea in a boat. A storm came up, and the disciples spent the night fighting against the wind and rain. They soon realized they were going nowhere, no matter how hard they tried. By the time of the fourth watch, they realized that the storm was too much for them. And in this hour of desperation, Jesus came to the disciples. Jesus came in *the fourth watch of the night*, when it was darkest, when hopelessness was setting in, and when there was a sense of urgency.

[176] Richard Rohr, *Everything Belongs: The Gift of Contemplative Prayer* (New York: The Crossroad Publishing Company, 2003), 95.

[177] David Fraizer, "I Need You to Survive," copyright 2003, God's Music Inc./Li'l Dave's Music Inc., recorded by Hezekiah Walker.

ABOUT THE AUTHOR

BRENDA DARBY, with her MA from Biola University, is founder and president of IN HIS PRESENCE CENTER FOR SPIRITUAL TRANSFORMATION, a Christian organization designed to build spiritual mentors who promote unity and oneness in the world. As a member of SPIRITUAL DIRECTORS INTERNATIONAL and GRAFTED LIFE MINISTRIES, she is a nurturer at heart, and her ministry extends from the shores of the Pacific Ocean to the continent of Africa. She is a Christian Spiritual Guide and follower of Ruth Haley Barton, Henri Nouwen, and Howard Thurman. Brenda is available for speaking engagements across a variety of Spiritual Formation, racial issues, and other topics that promote unity in the faith. Brenda can be reached at ihpcare@gmail.com.

Made in the USA
Las Vegas, NV
01 January 2024

83776569R00121